MCDONNELL DOUGLAS

LEGENDS OF FLIGHT

DOUGLAS DC-9

A Legends of Flight Illustrated History

WOLFGANG BORGMANN

SCHIFFER MILITARY
4880 Lower Valley Road Atglen, PA 19310

FSC
www.fsc.org
MIX
Paper from responsible sources
FSC® C104723

Other Schiffer books by the author
McDonnell Douglas DC-10/MD-11: A Legends of Flight Illustrated History, ISBN: 978-0-7643-6137-1
Boeing 707: A Legends of Flight Illustrated History, ISBN: 978-0-7643-6345-0
Boeing 737: A Legends of Flight Illustrated History, ISBN: 978-0-7643-6138-8

Other Schiffer books on related subjects
Boeing 757: A Legends of Flight Illustrated History, Dan Dornseif, ISBN: 978-0-7643-6346-7

Originally published as *Die Flugzeugstars: Douglas DC-9* by Motorbuch Verlag © 2018 Motorbuch Verlag
Translated from the German by David Johnston

Library of Congress Control Number: 2022932056

Cover design by Molly Shields
Type set in DIN/Minion Pro

ISBN: 978-0-7643-6484-6
Printed in China

Published by Schiffer Publishing, Ltd.
4880 Lower Valley Road
Atglen, PA 19310
Phone: (610) 593-1777; Fax: (610) 593-2002
Email: Info@schifferbooks.com
Web: www.schifferbooks.com

CONTENTS

Twenty-one examples of the C-9A Nightingale, based on the DC-9-30, were delivered to the US Air Force beginning in 1968. *NASA*

88934
UNITED STATES AIR FORCE

INTRODUCTION

DREAM NO SMALL DREAM; IT LACKS MAGIC. DREAM LARGE. THEN MAKE THE DREAM REAL.

—Donald Douglas Jr.

At the beginning of the 1970s, the fleet operated by LTU, the former charter airline from Dusseldorf, consisted of SE 210s and Fokker F-28s. *LTU*

When Douglas began initial planning for a twin-engine short-range and midrange jet airliner in 1963, its competition resided not in the US, as might have been expected, but in Europe. The French company Sud Aviation had flown the prototype of its SE 210 Caravelle in 1955, and it was to serve as the inspiration for many subsequent jet designs. The next evolutionary step was taken by Hunting Aircraft Company of Great Britain, whose BAC 111 first flew in 1963. These were, at least in the Western world, the only available twin-engine jet airliners that Douglas had to vie with for the favor of the airlines. The Boeing executive board did not decide to produce the Boeing 737, which is so taken for granted today, until 1965, by which time the first Douglas DC-9 was already flying.

Looking back, both the DC-9 and the later Boeing 737 owe much of their success to their power plants. Pratt & Whitney had created a true masterpiece with its JT8D engine. In its various versions, the JT8D has provided the necessary thrust for the DC-9 series, from the original version with a maximum takeoff weight of 90,389 pounds to the heaviest variant, the MD-83, with a maximum weight of 158,733 pounds. This was very much in contrast to the Rolls-Royce

LTU

Boarding an Austrian Airlines DC-9. *ETH-Bibliothek Zurich, Swissair*

This Swissair DC-9-32 displays the Douglas DC-9's design, perfected in the wind tunnel. *ETH-Bibliothek Zurich, Swissair*

Spey, which, in heavier versions of the BAC 111, barely produced sufficient thrust for takeoffs at high temperatures and from high elevations. The commitment of the British aviation industry to this national product led to truly bizarre tricks, especially when it came to the Hawker Siddeley HS 121 Trident 3B. In order to be able to take off in "hot and high" conditions with an economical payload, an additional power plant had to be added to the trijet, thus temporarily turning it into a four-engine jet. The Trident used this booster engine, which was also installed in the German Dornier Do 31 VTOL project, only for takeoff, after which it was nothing more than costly dead weight.

Thanks to the JT8D, Douglas was not forced to turn to these emergency solutions, and the Californian aircraft maker was always able to deliver the DC-9 variants desired by its customers. Early orders from Austrian Airlines, SAS, and Swissair meant that these three European airlines had considerable influence on the development of the range of DC-9 variants.

From the DC-9-21 to the DC-9-41 and DC-9-51 to the Model 81, these versions had their roots in the three partner airlines, which worked closely together for many years and—at the end of the 1990s—were even prepared to merge. Because of their importance to the development of the DC-9, this book gives them a lot of space. Other major customers, such as TWA and Delta Air Lines, basically purchased aircraft off the shelf. Not the Europeans, however, who traditionally have been willing to actively participate in the conception of the designs created for them through their own engineering directorates. The fact that this individualization did not always work in Douglas's favor is shown by the DC-9-21 and -41 variants tailored to the SAS route profile, of which only the latter found another buyer, in the shape of the Japanese domestic carrier TOA Domestic Airlines.

The design of the DC-9 with a T tail made it very popular with passengers, because the guests in the front rows of seats were almost completely spared the noise from the engines installed in the tail. The cockpit crews also benefited from this, since their workplace was so quiet that some airlines dispensed with the otherwise necessary headphones, and

SAS
KØBENHAVN COPENHAGEN
SAS
SAS
SAS
SAS
SAS

Hilton
Thai
SAS
SAS
SAS

The prominent nose of a Swissair DC-9. *ETH-Bibliothek Zurich, Swissair*

The MD-90 was powered by modern V2500 turbofan engines from the IAE consortium, made up of American engine maker Pratt & Whitney, the Aero Engine Corporation of Japan, and MTU Aero Engines of Germany. *SAS*

instructions from air traffic controllers were transmitted to the DC-9 cockpits via loudspeakers. However, this design also had its downsides: the aircraft's tail heaviness brought the DC-9 to its design limits at an early stage. The extended DC-9-41 had to carry ballast in the front cargo hold to ensure that a safe center-of-gravity range was maintained in flight when the load factor was low. This tendency toward tail heaviness also affected the later MD-80, MD-90, and MD-95 variants, whose engines were heavier than those of the original "classic" versions.

The DC-9's narrower fuselage compared to that of the 737, resulting in a maximum of five seats per row, was also popular with passengers. This meant that passengers on one side of the aisle were spared the unpopular middle seat, while on the side with three seats, the middle seats had to be occupied only at load factors of 80 percent and higher.

When McDonnell Douglas (MDD) launched the MD-80 in 1979, Boeing countered shortly afterward with the 737-300. In contrast to the CFM-56 engine of the successful jet from Seattle, the Pratt & Whitney JT8D-200 engine, which powered the MD-80, met the strictest noise criteria in force at the time, but in contrast to the CFM-56 it offered no further development prospects. McDonnell Douglas was thus forced to turn to the IAE V2500 for the stretched MD-90-30 and thus to offer a completely new engine for this type.

With the JT8D and the IAE V2500, loyal McDonnell Douglas customers already had to provide maintenance capacity and spare parts for two engine families, when McDonnell Douglas brought in an engine from a third manufacturer, the BMW Rolls-Royce BR 715, to power the MD-95. The family concept with which McDonnell Douglas had scored for three decades was now invalidated, and many former regular customers of the Californian manufacturer acknowledged this by switching to Boeing—and from 1987 onward to the Airbus A320 family. Financial difficulties as a result of poor sales of the MD-90 and MD-95 medium-haul jets and equally sluggish sales of the long-haul MD-11 finally led McDonnell Douglas to agree to a merger with archrival Boeing—which in retrospect looks more like a Boeing takeover. All of Long Beach's civil aircraft projects were

SCANDINAVIAN
SAS

discontinued in favor of the unchanged Boeing products from Seattle.

Nevertheless, the legendary DC-9 continues to fly to this day. Even some examples of the "Classic" versions from the 1960s and 1970s are still proving themselves in daily service, just like hundreds of MD-80s, MD-90s, and, above all, the MD-95 / Boeing 717s. The fact that many examples of the latter type are still in service in Australia and the USA – most of them flying for Delta Air Lines, even though production ended in May 2006, demonstrates the undiminished popularity of the successful model initiated by Donald Douglas Jr. and launched in 1965.

Wolfgang Borgmann
Oerlinghausen, summer 2022

The author's father, Herald Borgmann, in front of an SAS DC-9-41 at Stuttgart airport

Evening atmosphere at Basel-Mulhouse airport, which today markets itself as the Basel-Mulhouse-Freiburg region's EuroAirport. *ETH-Bibliothek Zurich, Swissair*

IFV
SWISSAIR
BALAIR

THE DC-9-21, IN PARTICULAR, HAD FLIGHT CHARACTERISTICS THAT WOULD DO HONOR TO A FIGHTER JET.

—Per-Olov Carlsson, last chief pilot on the SAS DC-9

MAERS
SAS

CHAPTER 1
THE HISTORY OF THE DOUGLAS DC-9

Thanks to its outstanding design, from the beginning of production in 1965 until it finally ended in 2006, the DC-9 was offered in countless versions, and for a time it was the most widely produced airliner in the world.

The managers of the Douglas Aircraft Company made initial investigations for a new short-and-medium-haul jet in 1958, almost simultaneously with the successful market entry by the company's DC-8 long-range airliner. The concept, whose internal Douglas designation was Model 2067, was initially envisaged as a smaller version of the DC-8, but the forty airline heads to whom company boss Donald Douglas Jr. personally wrote showed little interest in the small four-engine jet, whose dimensions would have been roughly similar to those of the Convair 880. A shoulder wing concept with four turboprop engines was also considered, but it likewise generated little interest. Uncertain whether the airlines would pay for a completely new

Previous double-page spread: MD-80s and MD-90s were a familiar sight on the ramp at Copenhagen airport in the 1990s. *Copenhagen Airports CPH*

Douglas and McDonnell Douglas civil aircraft, from the DC-1 to the DC-10-30. *SAS*

DC-1
TWA
DC-2
DC-3
LINJEFLYG
DC-4
SE-BBA
SWEDISH AIR LINES
DC-5
K·L·M
PH-AHL
DC-6
SCANDINAVIAN
DC-7
SAS
DC-8
SCANDINAVIAN
SAS
DC-9
SAS
SCANDINAVIAN
SE-DBS
DC-10
SCANDINAVIAN
SAS

In addition to DC-9-32s for short-haul routes, the airline Atlantis, once resident at Frankfurt, also operated the DC-8-63 on long-haul flights to the United States. *Atlantis*

development, Douglas initially shelved its own plans and instead entered into a cooperative arrangement with Sud Aviation, the French pioneer of the midrange jet airliner.

"Make good even better" could have been the motto of Douglas and Sud Aviation when the two aircraft makers signed a contract on February 10, 1960, for the joint development, production, and sale of the newly designed Series VII A of the proven SE 210 Caravelle. At first glance, cooperation made sense for both partners. The American company gave Sud Aviation access to the largest commercial aviation market in the world, and Douglas could exploit Sud Aviation's years of experience building twin-engine jet airliners.

Within this cooperative effort, not only was Douglas to construct components for the joint project, it would also be responsible for technical support and the sale of the jointly offered Caravelle around the globe, with the exception of Europe and French-speaking countries. There were also plans to augment the production line in Toulouse in the south of France with a second at Douglas's Long Beach factory in California, in case the production rate should rise to exceed eight aircraft per month.

The partners selected General Electric CJ805-23C turbofan engines to power the aircraft. A modified form of this engine was also installed in the Convair 990 Coronado four-engine airliner.

As part of this "Americanization" of its successful aircraft design, Sud Aviation developed new cockpit windows, whose larger design met all the requirements of the American FAA with respect to the pilots' view from the cockpit. As well, the fuselage was stretched by about 3.3 feet compared to the SE 210 III basic model, and the wings were aerodynamically refined.

However, all the sales efforts by the transatlantic partners led to just one order—partly financed by Douglas itself—from Trans World Airlines (TWA) for twenty Douglas–Sud Aviation Caravelles. Like so many earlier aircraft types, TWA initially showed great interest in the Caravelle but then decided in favor of a competing design—in this case the Boeing 727. Thus, apart from a single test bed financed by GE, the American-French SE 210 remained nothing more than an initially vague but in the end unfulfilled hope. After Douglas and Sud Aviation cordially ended their cooperative effort in

1961, the French manufacturer offered the aircraft, now called the SE 210 Horizon or Super Caravelle, whose prototype flew for the first time on August 31, 1962, on its own. Sud Aviation failed to sell a single example, however.

After this French interlude, Douglas turned once again to its own development of a short-range-and-midrange jet under the designation Project 2086, which was offered to the airlines from October 1961. The 2086 was initially conceived to transport a maximum of seventy-seven passengers and their luggage over a distance of about 620 miles (1,000 kilometers). From the outset, however, Douglas envisaged the development of larger versions and ultimately designed the DC-9, which resulted from that project study, with great development potential.

In January 1962, Donald Douglas Jr., then president of the Douglas Aircraft Company, met with teams of potential launch customers. Six North American airlines, including Eastern, American, Trans-Canada, Delta, National, and Continental, all showed great interest in the DC-9, as did the Australian operators Trans Australia Airlines (TAA) and Ansett.

They were unanimously impressed by the medium-haul jet with its distinctive T tail offered by Douglas; however, they criticized the choice of the relatively inefficient Pratt & Whitney JTF-10 engine. Douglas took the airlines' criticisms seriously and decided in favor of the more powerful Pratt & Whitney JT8D as the standard power plant, which in its numerous variants was to become "the" power plant for American medium-haul jets in the 1960s and 1970s. The JT8D engine alone was an important sales argument for the DC-9 in comparison to the British BAC 111, which was almost the same size. The DC-9's Anglo-Saxon competitor suffered on account of its Rolls-Royce Spey engines, which barely provided sufficient thrust, especially in the stretched versions of the BAC 111.

Although the DC-9 rose to temporarily become the most produced jetliner of all time in the 1990s—a title that is now owned by the Boeing 737—when the program was launched, its prospects did not look very promising. It was not until a month after the go-ahead that Delta placed the first meager order for fifteen aircraft. That same year, orders followed from Bonanza Air Lines and Trans-Canada Airlines for three and six aircraft, respectively. Swissair's order for ten DC-9-15s on May 13, 1964, was another milestone, as was the signing of a contract for twenty DC-9-14s by TWA president Charles Tillinghast on July 20 of that year. It was not until 1965, however, that Douglas succeeded in sustainably filling the order books. In the period from the prototype's maiden flight in February of that year until the first DC-9-10 entered service with Delta Air Lines on December 8, Douglas's order backlog rose from 58 to 228 aircraft.

THE DC-9 TAKES OFF

Production of the DC-9 officially began on July 26, 1963, with the beginning of structural work. The first sets of wings were delivered by Canadian partner company De Havilland Aircraft of Canada Ltd. from its factory in Malton, Ontario, in January 1964, while Douglas was working on the first fuselages at Long Beach. At the same time, Douglas used its high-speed wind tunnel to optimize the aircraft design created by some one thousand engineers.

The first flight by the prototype on February 25, 1965, from the Douglas factory in Long Beach to Edwards Air Force Base, was followed by an intensive flight test program in which up to five aircraft took part.

In contrast to the other jetliners equipped with a T tail, the DC-9 test crews were spared fatal accidents. On account of its design, the DC-9 also ran the risk of entering a "locked-in or deep stall." This causes a complete loss of control of the aircraft when the T tail's elevator and rudder become virtually ineffective at low speeds and a high angle of attack. Despite all precautionary measures taken in advance, prototypes of the comparable BAC 111, Hawker Siddeley 121 Trident, and Hamburger Flugzeugbau HFB 320 Hansa Jet all crashed during testing.

As an effective countermeasure, all affected types are equipped with "stick shaker" and "stick pusher" systems, which initially issue warnings to the pilots acoustically, visually, and by shaking the control yoke before they reach the critical flight condition, and if these are not heeded, they automatically push the control column forward.

Alarmed, particularly by the crash of the BAC 111 prototype on October 23, 1963, Douglas also implemented a series of design measures to prevent a similar accident befalling the DC-9, by improving the aerodynamic design of the aircraft. These included changes to the wing and larger horizontal tail surfaces with an approximately 23 percent increase in area.

DC-9-10

The first delivery to Delta Air Lines was followed within a few months by the first DC-9-10s for Continental, Eastern, and TWA, with which they offered jet comfort even on less frequented routes. Continental was also the first customer for the DC-9-15 RC (Rapid Change) version, with a side cargo door on the main deck, which could be converted from a passenger aircraft to a freighter—and back—within seventy-five minutes. A mixed passenger-freight version was also possible, with a partition separating the cargo area and the passenger cabin. To facilitate rapid configuration changes, the passenger seats and kitchen module were mounted on pallets.

A total of 137 Douglas DC-9-10s left the factory buildings at Long Beach between 1965 and 1968, the final example being handed over to Aeronaves de Mexico on March 27, 1968.

As popular as this first variant of the DC-9 initially was, the first customers quickly parted with their DC-9-10s as soon as larger versions with stretched fuselages became available, offering the prospect of lower costs per seat.

DC-9-30

Douglas found itself in the comfortable position of being able to quickly offer a stretched version of the DC-9 basic model. From the beginning, the aircraft had been designed for this possibility, and its Pratt & Whitney JT8D turbofan engines also offered great development potential—they had been derated to a maximum of 12,000 pounds thrust for takeoff for the DC-9-10 basic version. When Douglas required a more powerful engine for the DC-9-20 stretched version, an optimal power plant was immediately available in the JT8D-7. Thanks to its stretched fuselage, which was lengthened by 15 feet (4.57 meters), five additional rows of seats could be installed in the DC-9-30, increasing maximum seating capacity from eighty (DC-9-10) to 115 seats.

An illustration published by Iberia in the 1970s illustrating a DC-9-10 in its livery. In fact, however, the Spanish airline operated only Series 30 DC-9s. *Iberia*

Charter airline Aero Lloyd's DC-9-32 with the registration D-ALLB was originally built for the Indonesian airline Garuda in 1975 and was finally operated by the Mexican airline Aero California until 2008. *Aero Lloyd*

A DC-9-41 on final approach to Copenhagen-Kastrup airport. The airport is on the Öresund, the strait that separates Denmark and Sweden. *SAS*

This most popular version of the DC-9, with a total of 662 examples sold, was certified by the FAA on December 16, 1966, and deliveries to launch customer Eastern Air Lines began in January 1967. Very much in the Douglas tradition, the Series 30 was available in a wide range of equipment variants; for example, as a freighter, passenger-cargo combi version, air-ambulance version for the American military, and various range and power plant versions.

The DC-9 was the first model of the "Douglas commercial" series procured by the American Department of Defense since the DC-6 (C-118). After the military restarted the numbering of its aircraft types in 1962 beginning from "1," the military transport version of the DC-9 was assigned the number "9" as the ninth type ordered. It was by good fortune rather than planning that the military version of the DC-9 became the C-9. Structurally, the C-9, which was used almost exclusively in the aeromedical evacuation role, was identical to the DC-9-30.

The differences between the versions lay in the oxygen system, the electrical system, and the cabin, which had been optimized for medical purposes. In addition to the two pilots, the typical crew of a Douglas C-9 consisted of a medical crew director, two flight nurses, and three aeromedical technicians. Their task was to operate the flying aid station's complex instruments and systems. Litter-borne patients could be brought on board using a hydraulically operated ramp. Patients requiring isolation or intensive care were accommodated in a special-care area with a separate ventilation system and constant temperature and humidity levels. The C-9 also has a decontamination station for various warfare agents.

Twenty-one aircraft were delivered to the US Air Force starting in 1968 as the C-9A Nightingale, while from 1973 onward, the US Navy received twelve examples called the C-9B Skytrain II, making it the successor to the famous C-47 Skytrain of the Second World War. Further purchases and the conversion of DC-9-32CFs caused the navy's fleet to temporarily grow to up to thirty aircraft. In 1976, the US Marine Corps took delivery of two new C-9B transports for use in the transport role.

SAS
SE-DBX

This photo of a C-9A Nightingale about to touch down shows the aircraft's leading-edge slats, which provided necessary lift during takeoff and landing. *NASA*

A US Air Force C-9A flying over St. Louis. Clearly visible is the city's symbol on the bank of the Mississippi River, the 192-meter-high Gateway Arch. *NASA*

For a time, DC-9s even flew as the US presidential Air Force One, after the Department of Defense ordered three VC-9Cs in December 1973, for use by government officials as VIP transports.

In addition to the US military, the armed forces of Kuwait received two C-9Bs purchased through the US Navy, while the Italian air force ordered two DC-9-32s as VIP transports. In addition, between 1977 and 1981, the Venezuelan air force leased a DC-9-15 for use as a military transport aircraft.

At the height of the Vietnam War, the US Navy seriously considered the purchase of a version of the C-9 suitable for carrier landings, with folding wings. This interesting project got no further than the design stage, however.

The final DC-9 "classic" built for an airline was a Series 31 with the construction number 1058, which was handed over to USAir at Long Beach on April 6, 1982. It was followed on October 28, 1982, by a US Navy C-9B, which was in fact the last DC-9 "classic" produced by McDonnell Douglas. Its delivery brought to a close a production run that had lasted seventeen years and was followed by the MD-80 and MD-90 programs, which continued for another twenty-four years.

68934
UNITED STATES AIR FORCE

McDonnell Douglas worked with its customers to adapt the design of the DC-9 passenger cabins to current tastes, so that they always looked modern to passengers. Cabin photo 1: The original cabin design of the 1960s and 1970s, with open hand luggage compartments above the passengers' heads. Cabin photo 2: The look of an SAS DC-9-41 at the time of its decommissioning in 2002. Curtains in the background visually separated the business and economy classes and could be moved between the seat rows depending on the booking situation. Cabin photos 3 and 4: Designed by the Austrian company Fischer in the 1990s, the cabin of the MD-95/Boeing 717 still has a modern look today.

DC-9-41

Both Swissair of Switzerland and SAS of Scandinavia were longtime Douglas customers. While the Swiss began operating their first Douglas product, the DC-2, in 1934, the three founding companies of the SAS consortium, founded in 1946, brought a large number of DC-3 Dakotas and DC-4 Skymasters into the trinational airline merger. Both Swissair and SAS flew all of the successful Douglas designs produced until the end of the 1950s—the DC-4, DC-6, DC-6B, DC-7C, and DC-8-32.

When Swissair finally ordered the DC-9-10 in 1965, it was only a question of time until SAS followed the example of its then-close technical and commercial partner.

However, neither the DC-9-10 nor the Series 30, which was stretched by 4.57 meters (15 feet), met the Scandinavians' requirements with respect to range and passenger capacity. SAS was seeking a suitable replacement for its SE 210 III Caravelle fleet, which it had placed in service just six years earlier, the first airline anywhere in the world to do so. At the end of the 1950s the Caravelle was regarded as a technical sensation, but advances in aircraft design in the few years until 1965 came at a rapid pace. Compared to the SE 210, the further-developed BAC 111, Boeing 727, and DC-9 all offered the ability to transport greater payloads at significantly lower operating costs.

Douglas finally made SAS a tempting offer. The Americans were prepared to produce a version of the DC-9 specifically for the airline. With a fuselage lengthened by an additional 6.3 feet (1.92 meters) compared to the DC-9-30, the resulting DC-9-41 was designed to carry a maximum of 125 passengers. On January 25, 1966, the "Flying Vikings" placed an initial order for ten examples of "their" DC-9. Compared to the Caravelle, the DC-9-41 could carry up to an additional eighteen passengers and 459 cubic feet (13 cubic meters) of cargo—and that with a 52.8-gallon-per-hour (200 liter per hour) saving in fuel consumption.

The first DC-9-41 tailored for SAS, with the name "Hemming Viking" and the registration OY-KGA, arrived in Scandinavia on February 29, 1968, and one month later entered service on the Copenhagen-to-Stockholm route. SAS ordered a total of forty-nine examples of this type, several of which were leased to Swissair and to Thai Airways International, which had been founded by SAS. The specialization of this DC-9 version for the SAS route network may have been the reason why the only other customer to order it was Toa Domestic Airlines of Japan, which purchased twenty-two DC-9-41s for its inland network. Production ended after seventy-one aircraft had been completed. Not until 1991 did the enterprising SAS managers sell their oldest DC-9-41 to Northwest Airlines for eight million dollars—3.5 million dollars more than they had paid for the aircraft in 1968.

DC-9-21

While the DC-9-41 proved a success in service on SAS's European routes, the Scandinavians faced the task of finding a replacement for their Convair CV 440 propeller-driven aircraft. In the late 1960s, these airliners, called Metropolitans, were used mainly on Scandinavian inland routes, since they were the only aircraft in the entire SAS fleet that could operate from the very short runways of many northern provincial airports.

The British BAC 111 was already on the shortlist when, for a second time, Douglas made an irresistible offer. The hybrid it offered combined the short fuselage of the DC-9-10 with the larger wings and more-powerful engines of the DC-9-41.

The resulting DC-9-21 was, as one can easily imagine, a real powerhouse. It was capable of taking off with a full payload and flying to Oslo, even from the short 5,249-foot (1,600 meter) runways of Norwegian airports north of the Arctic Circle. It is no wonder that SAS pilots were soon calling it the DC-9 "Sport" on account of its extraordinary performance. However, SAS purchased this specialization at the price of extremely high costs per seat-kilometer. The DC-9-21 filled its purpose in Scandinavia, but production was limited to just the ten examples built specially for SAS.

The DC-9-21 illustrated here had the same dimensions as the DC-9-10, and the main external difference between the two variants was the former's leading-edge slats. *SAS*

The DC-9 required external passenger stairs only if there was a technical problem with its two sets of integral stairs, on the port side of the forward fuselage and in the tail of the aircraft. The latter can be seen in the photo of a Swissair DC-9 on the facing page. *Hamburg Airport*

The DC-9 required external passenger stairs only if there was a technical problem with its two sets of integral stairs, on the port side of the forward fuselage and in the tail of the aircraft. The latter can be seen in the photo of a Swissair DC-9 on the facing page. *ETH-Bibliothek Zurich, Swissair*

SCANDINAVIAN
UBBE VIKING
SAS

The DC-9-21 with the aircraft name Ubbe Viking was one of ten examples of this type to be produced. The aircraft entered service with SAS in 1969. *SAS*

Takeoff by an SAS DC-9-21 in the airline's pre-1980s livery. *SAS*

Swissair was the launch customer for the DC-9-51 version. *ETH-Bibliothek Zurich, Swissair*

The last example of this DC-9 variant did not leave the SAS fleet until October 2000, almost thirty-two years after the first aircraft entered service.

DC-9-51

The Swiss airline Swissair was the launch customer for this last version marketed exclusively as a "DC-9," before McDonnell Douglas took another major step in the evolution basic DC-9 design with the MD-80 and MD-90 families of aircraft. Compared to the DC-9-10 basic model, the Series 51, announced by Douglas in July 1973, had a fuselage stretched by 29.2 feet (8.89 meters) and more-powerful Pratt & Whitney JT8D-17 power plants. The first flight by the biggest DC-9 "classic" version took place at Long Beach on December 17, 1974. A total of twelve DC-9-51s, which were certified to carry a maximum of 139 passengers, were flown by Swissair beginning on August 24, 1975. Other important European customers for this type were Austrian Airlines, Inex Adria, and Finnair. Douglas produced a total of ninety-six examples of the DC-9-51 between 1975 and 1981.

THE NASA DC-9 "REFAN" PROGRAM

At the beginning of the 1970s, ecological awareness was growing around the globe, and the fight against aircraft noise pollution became increasingly important. Douglas responded in 1972, together with Pratt & Whitney and Rohr Industries, which made the DC-9's engine nacelles, by means of a program to actively reduce aircraft noise at its source—the engines. In addition to supplying retrofit kits, starting in 1973 all DC-9s were delivered with these quieter JT8D engines as standard.

As if that were not enough, the American air and space agency NASA promoted the development of a JT8D engine with a larger fan diameter, which promised more power with less noise and lower fuel consumption. A corresponding agreement to build two of these engines, designated the JT8D-109, was signed in July 1973 among McDonnell Douglas, NASA, and Pratt & Whitney. The DC-9 was ideally suited for the planned flight tests, since an alternative installation of engines with their large fan diameter under the wings of the Boeing 737 or in the squat tail of the Boeing 727 would have been more difficult. The two fans at the front of the original JT8D engine, with a diameter of 3.38 feet (1.03 meters), were replaced by a single fan measuring 4.1 feet (1.25 meters) diagonally.

The first flight of the "Refan" DC-9-32 took place on January 9, 1975. The flight test program, which lasted around ninety hours, was completed over a period of three months from Yuma, Arizona.

Parallel to this, wind tunnel tests were carried out at NASA's Lewis Research Center in Cleveland, Ohio. After completion of the flight tests, the DC-9 was reequipped with its original JT8D-9 engines in March 1975 and sold to Yugoslavian Inex Adria Airways in 1976. Even though the JT8D-109 engine did not go into production, these trials paved the way for the more powerful JT8D-200 engine—and thus to the DC-9-80.

Artist's impression of the DC-9 Refan with its two experimental Pratt & Whitney JT8D-109 engines. *NASA*

The modified DC-9-32 during one its many test flights over the Arizona desert. *NASA*

The fan of the experimental JT8D-109 engine was 22 percent larger than that of the standard JT8D-9 engine. *NASA*

Graphic depiction of DC-9 development—from the Series 10 of 1965 to the DC-9-81, which took off on its maiden flight in October 1979. *McDonnell Douglas*

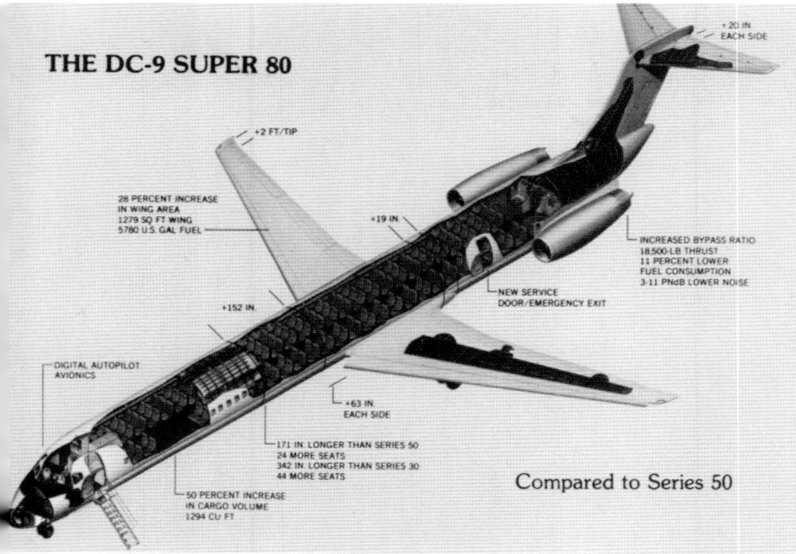

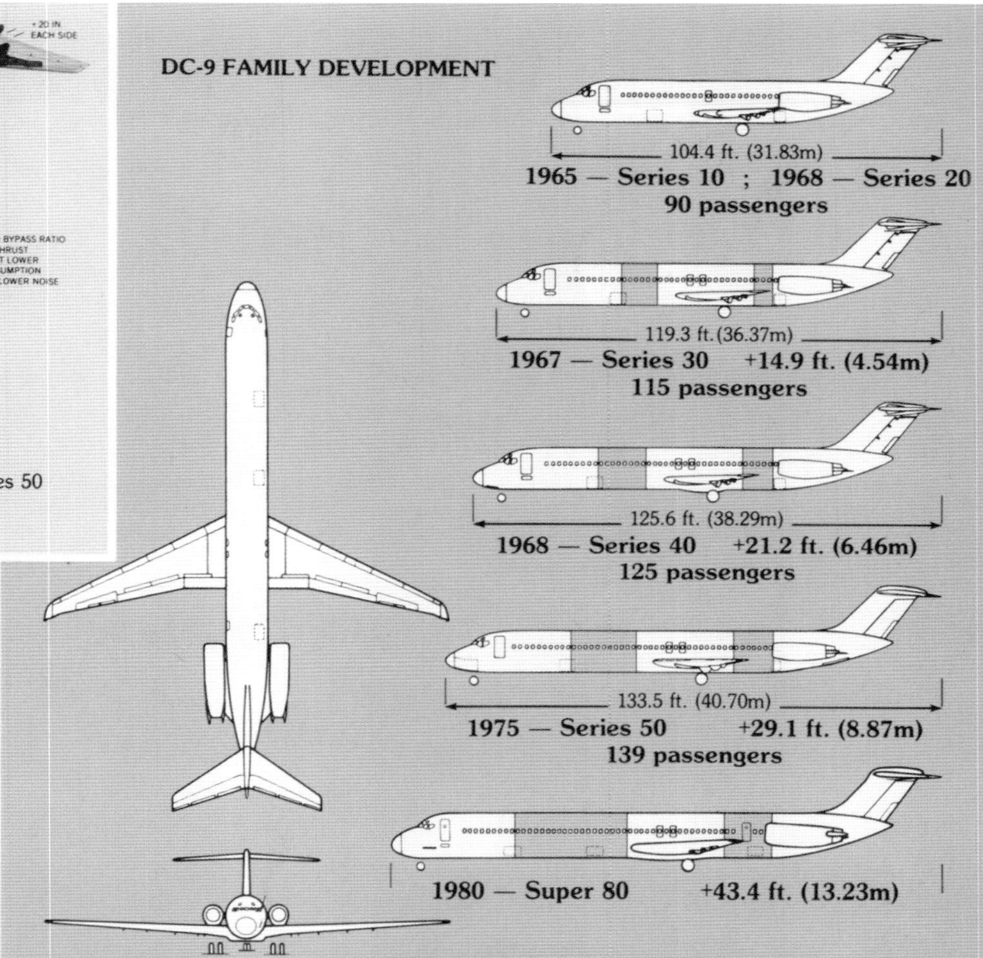

The McDonnell Douglas Super 80, the sixth basic model in the pendable DC-9 family of twinjet transports, was designed to ease e severe operating problems confronting the airline industry, while ntinuing DC-9 standards of excellence in the transportation of ssengers and cargo over short to medium range routes.

The newest and largest model in the popular DC-9 twinjet transport ries, the Super 80 was designed to confront the environmental, onomic, and energy problems of airline operators now and in the xt decade.

Environment: A blend of new and mature technology, the Super is the world's quietest commercial jetliner in service with the major lines. The reduced noise levels of the Super 80 make it a very "good ighbor" to airport communities everywhere.

Economy: Because of its advanced, high technology, turbofan gines, its higher capacity fuselage with its roomy, comfortable bin, and its larger, more efficient, higher aspect ratio wing, the per 80's operating costs are the lowest of any aircraft in its class.

Energy: Its fuel consumption per passenger is the lowest for any mmercial jet transport in its size category, or larger. The Super 80 designed to carry 137 passengers and their baggage more than 00 statute miles (3,219 km) nonstop. Its maximum seating is 172.

n the Super 80, McDonnell Douglas is producing a twinjet that carry more passengers and cargo farther, from shorter runways, d at lower seat mile costs, while offering the same passenger appeal d reliability of its other DC-9 transport aircraft.

By June 1981, McDonnell Douglas had delivered more than 983 C-9s in all versions.

Super 80 Specifications

length:	147.8 ft. (45.06 m)	**cruise speed:**	546 mph (879 km/hr.)
height:	29.7 ft. (9.05 m)	**range:** (approximately)	1,600 st. mi. (2,575 km) (or) 2,000 st. mi. (3,219 km)
wing span:	107.8 ft. (32.87 m)	**passenger capacity:**	137-172
propulsion:	2 Pratt & Whitney JT8D-209 turbofan engines, 18,500 lbs. (8,392 kg) thrust each (or) JT8D-217 turbofan engines, 20,000 lbs. (9,072 kg) thrust each.	**crew:**	2 plus cabin attendants
		first flight:	18 October 1979
		first airline delivery:	Swissair, 12 September 1980

The prototype DC-9-81 taking off from Long Beach on its maiden flight on October 18, 1979. *McDonnell Douglas*

The DC-9-81 cuts a good figure from any perspective, here during pushback at Copenhagen airport. *SAS*

DC-9-81 (MD-81)

Officially launched in October 1977, with orders from Swissair and Austrian Airlines, the DC-9-81 version was much more than a stretched version of the basic model. The changes implemented in the DC-9 "Super 80" included larger wings with an improved high-lift system, an enlarged tailplane, new cockpit instrumentation, a wide-body-look passenger cabin, and, last but not least, Pratt & Whitney JT8D-200 engines, used for the first time on the DC-9 with a new, larger fan to increase power and reduce noise. Since the first flight of the DC-9 prototype in 1965, the JT8D has also been the standard engine of a number of other jets, such as the Boeing 727, Boeing 737, and Dassault Mercure. By the early 1990s, there were some 12,000 JT8Ds in service around the globe, making it the most widely used civil jet engine at the time. A comparison of the original JT8D-1 version from 1961, with a maximum thrust of 14,000 lbs. (62.28 kN), and the final JT8D-219 version, with a maximum thrust of 21,000 lbs. (93.42 kN), illustrates the development potential of this engine.

The DC-9-81 basic version, marketed by McDonnell Douglas as the MD-80 from 1983 onward, received certification from the US Federal Aviation Administration (FAA) on August 26, 1980. Swissair, the launch customer, commenced service between Zurich and Frankfurt on October 5 of that year.

DC-9-82 (MD-82)

In April 1979, McDonnell Douglas announced the MD-82, an improved version of the MD-80 family. Externally identical to the DC-9-81, the MD-82 differs mainly in its more powerful Pratt & Whitney JT8D-217 engines. Production of the MD-82, which made its maiden flight on January 8, 1981, totaled 569 aircraft and was second only to the DC-9-30 as the most popular DC-9 variant. The MD-82 was certified by the FAA on July 30, 1981, and entered service with its launch customer, Republic Airlines, in August of that year. This order for fourteen aircraft was initially in limbo after Republic experienced significant financial difficulties in 1981. For this reason, the airline, which had merged with Hughes Airwest only a year earlier, was able to take delivery of only three of the MD-82s it had ordered from the manufacturer.

In addition to the brand-new MD-82s, numerous MD-81s were retrofitted to MD-82 standard.

DC-9-83 (MD-83)

Specially designed for long distances and takeoffs in hot climates and from high-elevation airfields, with its two JT8D-219 engines producing 21,000 pounds (93.42 kN) of thrust for takeoff, the MD-83 was equipped with the most powerful variant of the Pratt & Whitney engine. In addition, its maximum takeoff weight had been increased to 160,937 lbs. (73 metric tons), and fuel capacity was further increased by the installation of a 1,160-US-gallon (4,390 liter) center fuel tank. This version of the DC-9, which first flew on December 17, 1984, was initially operated by Finnair and Alaska Airlines. In Germany, MD-83s were flown by the charter airline Aero Lloyd and the short-lived scheduled airline German Wings—not to be confused with today's Lufthansa subsidiary of the same name. The first German Wings offered flights within Germany and to Paris in 1989 and 1990, in competition with Lufthansa. The MD-83s were configured with just 114 seats in a pure business-class layout with a 2+2 seat arrangement per row. Even on domestic flights, each passenger received a hot meal during the flight. The concept failed—not least due to the fierce competition from Lufthansa—which in 2008 acquired the rights to the German Wings word-image trademark, but not the insolvent company.

Along with Swissair, Austrian Airlines was an early customer for the DC-9-81.
Austrian Airlines

Swissair received its first DC-9-81 on September 12, 1980. *Swissair*

The European Quality Alliance (EQA) of the late 1980s and early 1990s could also be referred to as the "MD-80 airlines club." At that time, Austrian Airlines, Finnair, SAS, and Swissair all exclusively operated Douglas DC-9s and MD-80s on their European routes covered by EQA. The customers of the individual alliance airlines benefited from the ability to check in with one airline to the destination of an EQA partner, receive their boarding pass at airline counters in selected hotels, check their baggage there, and use the business-class lounges of all the partners. In addition, at major airports such as London Heathrow, the partners concentrated their operation in a common terminal. *SAS*

Illustration from German charter airline Aero Lloyd postcard, promoting flights on its MD-83s. *Aero Lloyd*

Copenhagen airport was a mecca for MD-80 fans in the 1980s. *SAS*

Like with the DC-9 aircraft, advancements were also made in simulator technology for the training of cockpit crews. While in the early years crews had to rely on static-procedure trainers, with no visual representation of the outside world, by the 1980s modern MD-80 all-axis simulators (*left*) were providing a realistic flight experience. *ETH-Bibliothek Zurich, Swissair*

COOPERATION WITH CHINA

McDonnell Douglas (MDD) was a pioneer in aircraft-manufacturing cooperation with the People's Republic of China. Long before Airbus, McDonnell Douglas signed an agreement with the Chinese aerospace industry on April 12, 1985, for the production, initially, of twenty-five MD-82 aircraft under license in China. Components prefabricated in China and the United States were assembled at the final-assembly site in Shanghai beginning in 1986. The first aircraft produced in Shanghai for the then Chinese national airline CAAC flew for the first time on July 2, 1987. Just one month later it began flying on Chinese domestic routes. Within the framework of this first American-Chinese cooperative effort in civil aircraft construction, thirty-five MD-82s were produced.

As if that were not enough, McDonnell Douglas and the National Aero-Technology Import/Export Corporation (CATIC) reached another agreement in 1992 to produce up to forty MD-80s and MD-90s in the People's Republic of China. Because of their planned use on "trunk routes," the aircraft were called "TrunkLiners." After the planned export of US high-tech production facilities to the People's Republic of China initially met with suspicion on the part of the US government, the partners amended the contract so that of the forty aircraft, just twenty MD-90s would be produced in China and twenty other MD-80s would be delivered directly from MDD in Long Beach. In fact, the US government's fears came true, since some of the production equipment delivered to China did not find its way into MD-90 production but ended up in factories producing Chinese fighter jets. In the end, just two MD-90-30T "TrunkLiners" were produced in Shanghai, since MDD had ended the supply of materials to the Chinese final-assembly line after its merger with Boeing.

As for the MD-90 production facilities that had remained in China, they were subsequently used for production of the Comac ARJ21 regional jet, developed and produced in Shanghai, whose wings were developed from scratch by the Ukrainian Antonov Design Bureau. With its CF34 engines from General Electric and cockpit instrumentation from Rockwell Collins, the ARJ21 has a large US share in the overall program. And since its fuselage structure is identical to that of the MD-90, at least part of the "good old DC-9" will continue to fly in the future, carrying the hopes of the Chinese aviation industry.

DC-9-87

The DC-9-87 was the first version of the MD-80 family whose fuselage was shortened again. Announced by Douglas in January 1985, the MD-87 was popular among existing and new DC-9 customers primarily because of its increased range. The first aircraft took to the air at Long Beach on December 4, 1986, while the first production aircraft entered service with launch customer Austrian Airlines on December 17, 1987. Finnair followed shortly after. The seventy-five examples built served not only with airlines but also as business jets.

A Balair MD-87 taking off from Zurich airport. *ETH-Bibliothek Zurich, Swissair*

SCANDINAVIAN
SE-DIC
SAS

The first MD-87 took off on its maiden flight on December 4, 1986. *SAS*

The original cockpit of a Swissair DC-9-81, which closely resembled that of the DC-9 "Classic," compared to the modern glass cockpit of an SAS MD-82. *ETH-Bibliothek Zurich, Swissair / SAS*

MD-88

The MD-88, of which 150 examples were built, was the first aircraft in the series that was not certified as the "Douglas Commercial" DC-9 but as the McDonnell Douglas MD-80 series. The MD-88 differed from its sisters the MD-81, MD-82, and MD-83 primarily in the first factory installation of a so-called glass cockpit. In addition to the new display screens for the pilot, the upgrade also included a computer-based flight management system. The new systems not only reduced pilot workload but also ensured more-precise adherence to flight paths and more economical planning and execution of the flight. The first customer for this most technologically advanced version of the MD-80 was Delta Air Lines, which launched the MD-88 program with an order for eighty aircraft. The first MD-88 flew on August 15, 1987, and the type entered service with Delta on January 5, 1988. McDonnell Douglas also offered the possibility of retrofitting older models of the MD-80 family to MD-88 standard. SAS of Scandinavia was one of the companies that took advantage of this opportunity.

During its production life from 1980 to 1999, 1,191 aircraft of all versions of the MD-80 series were delivered by McDonnell Douglas.

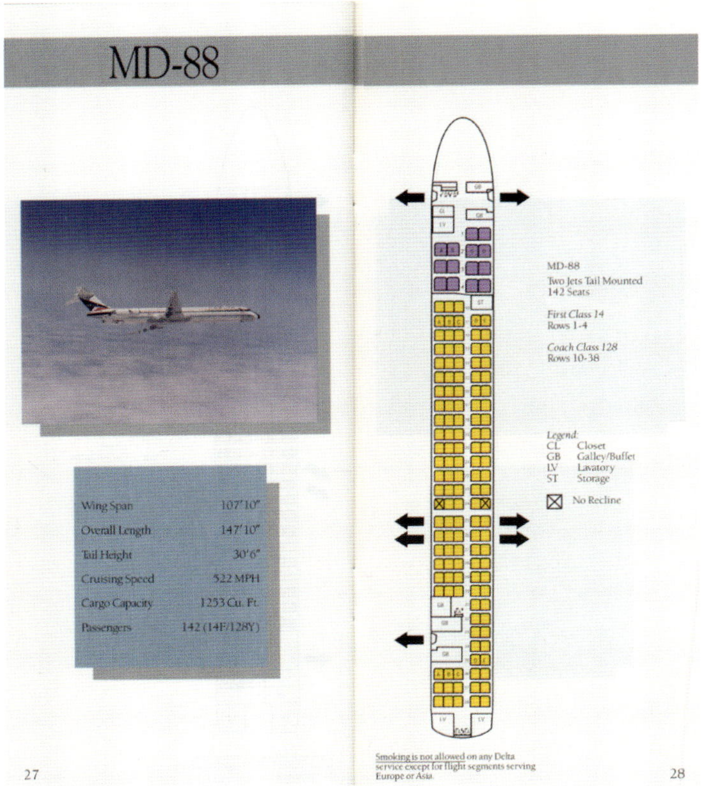

Delta Air Lines MD-88 seating plan. *Delta Air Lines*

Delta Air Lines was the first customer for the McDonnell Douglas MD-88, a further development of the DC-9 equipped with a so-called glass cockpit and a modern flight management system. *Delta Air Lines*

MD-90

On November 14, 1989, McDonnell Douglas presented its MD-90 aircraft family as the newest development of the MD-80 series, which was in turned based on the original DC-9 design from the 1960s. The MD-90-10, -30, and -40 were three types designed to carry 110, 150, and 180 passengers in a two-class configuration. The MD-90-20 designation was reserved for a version of the MD-80 whose Pratt & Whitney JT8D-200 engines were to be retroactively replaced with quieter and more economical International Aero Engines (IAE) V2500s, the standard power plants of the MD-90.

By the time the first MD-90-30 entered service with Delta Air Lines, McDonnell Douglas was already in serious financial turmoil. Two years later, the merger with Boeing followed, and thus the creeping end of most Douglas models.

For the MD-90 program, which was in competition with the better-selling Boeing 737 "Next Generation" types within the new American aviation company, the merger with Boeing meant the ultimate end in 2000 after 116 aircraft had been completed. The projected MD-90-10, -20, and -40 series were not built. Only the MD-95, a separate project from the DC-9/MD-80, remained in production until 2006 and remains very popular to this day as the Boeing 717 regional jet.

An SAS MD-90-30 on a test flight in the United States prior to delivery to the Scandinavian airline. SAS

MD-95

The MD-95 project goes back to initial plans by McDonnell Douglas (MDD) in 1983 for a shortened version of the DC-9-81. The DC-9-90 model was to have a maximum capacity of 117 seats and was primarily intended for the then-expanding US air transport market. With the close involvement of Northwest Airlines, the program matured until MDD partnered with Pratt & Whitney and the China Aero-Technology Import/Export Corporation (CATIC) at the Paris Air Show in 1991 to develop a 105-seat version of the MD-80 for delivery in 1995 at the earliest. Initially designated the MD-87-105, the aircraft was to be pursued closely with existing Chinese partners, with whom MDD already was already cooperating on the TrunkLiner and MD-90 programs. As alternative power plants, McDonnell initially offered the Pratt & Whitney JT8D-218 and Rolls-Royce Tay 670 turbofan engines.

In July 1994, the McDonnell Douglas board of directors approved the new MD-95, which was structurally based on the DC-9-30, designed in 1966. From the outset, the manufacturer focused on low production costs in order to make the aircraft attractive to low-cost airlines. MDD therefore limited itself to the final assembly of the components produced by a global network of suppliers. The Italian company Alenia produced the fuselages; Hyundai Space and Aircraft of South Korea, the wings; Korean Aerospace, also of South Korea, the nose; and British Aerospace, the tail.

The McDonnell Douglas Long Beach plant was first awarded the final assembly of the MD-95 after the unions and the state of California agreed to financial concessions.

In March 1995, in the midst of preparations for the official program launch, the news burst that Scandinavian Airlines System (SAS), which had been a loyal customer for decades and was also a firm buyer of the MD-95, had ordered the Boeing 737-600, the competing product from Boeing. The SAS order for the small jet from Seattle had a fatal signal effect in the global aviation market, and it was to be six months before the American low-cost airline ValuJet (AirTran) became the first customer to place its trust in the MD-95 on October 19, 1995, ordering fifty aircraft and signing an equal number of options for the type.

In the tradition of the Douglas jetliners, the MD-95 was designed to be safe, simple, easy to maintain, and reliable. The development team deviated from the DC-9 basic structure only when new materials and systems promised significant cost savings or improved aircraft reliability. As expected, the biggest structural changes were made in the tail to accommodate the large and heavy Rolls-Royce BR715 engines. Aside from the engines, the biggest difference from the DC-9 was the MD-95's cockpit avionics. It is a synthesis of Douglas and Boeing technologies and is based on the design of the MD-11 flight deck. The six LCD displays are based on screens originally developed by Honeywell for the Boeing 777 and used in the MD-10 upgrade program. Another new development was the passenger cabin, designed by the Austrian firm Fischer, which with then-modern materials and lighting systems gave the MD-95 a modern look on the inside as well.

In this drawing released by Boeing, the collaboration with BMW Rolls-Royce is highlighted through the display of their logos on the engine cowlings.
Boeing Commercial Airplane Group

717
T-1
A/C 5001
4

The 717 final-assembly line at Long Beach, California, with the first example of this type, shortly before its rollout. *Boeing Commercial Airplane Group*

Joe Corr, president and general manager of AirTran (*right*), and Gary Roberts, 717 production director, celebrate the beginning of final assembly of the first Boeing 717-200. *Boeing Commercial Airplane Group*

The 717 prototype on the factory floor of the former McDonnell Douglas production building, prior to painting and the official rollout ceremony on June 10, 1998. Boeing took over the factory in the summer of 1998. *Boeing Commercial Airplane Group*

The instrumentation in the cockpit of the MD-95 / Boeing 717 reflected the highest standards available in civic aircraft design in the late 1990s. *Boeing Commercial Airplane Group*

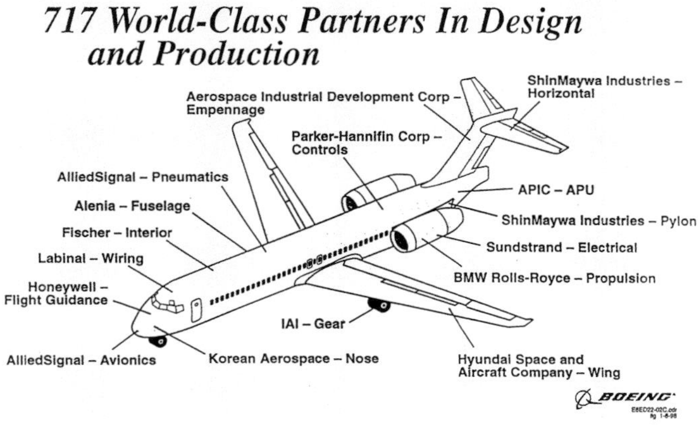

The Boeing 717 was produced by a global network of subcontractors, including some from Germany and Austria. Final assembly took place at the McDonnell Douglas / Boeing factory at Long Beach near Los Angeles. *Boeing Commercial Airplane Group*

Overall, the European aerospace industry had a value share in the Boeing 717 program of around 40 percent. Half of this was accounted for by the "high-bypass" turbofan engines built at the BMW Rolls-Royce plant in Dahlewitz, near Berlin, with a high bypass ratio for economical and quiet flight operations. In 1997, thirty years after the merger of Douglas and McDonnell, the financially troubled McDonnell Douglas Corporation merged with Boeing to form the world's largest aerospace company. Long Beach remained the site of the aircraft program now called the 717-200, which was symbolically presented to the public at the BMW Rolls-Royce plant in Dahlewitz on January 14, 1998, by Ron Woodard, president of the Boeing Commercial Airplane Group. This ceremony was not a premiere in the real sense, since McDonnell Douglas had already unveiled the identical regional jet as the MD-95 in October 1995. Rather, the project partners seemed to want to convey to the aviation industry in a promotional way that they still believed in the future of the aircraft program inherited from McDonnell Douglas.

The BR715 engine, manufactured in Dahlewitz, was the sole power plant offered for the 717. The official presentation of the new Boeing jetliner was also accompanied by the great hope that Dahlewitz, located in the eastern German state of Brandenburg, would establish itself as a production site for modern turbofan engines in the long term. Even after the Boeing 717 program did not develop as planned and BMW withdrew as a partner of Rolls-Royce in the year 2000, the British company not only held on to its German location but also invested sums of millions in its repeated expansion. The vague hopes of the engine builders in 1998 were thus completely fulfilled by nineteen years later.

Shattered dreams, however, were associated with the 717 regional jet, on whose economic success thousands of jobs at the traditional Douglas site in Long Beach depended, but even extensive marketing campaigns by the Boeing team had only limited success. After the first AirTran order, further orders came in slowly until the order book was closed after 156 orders.

It is an almost philosophical question whether the disastrous sales figures were to blame for the fact that the originally planned 717 family of aircraft was not produced—or the lack of this very family concept contributed to the low sales. The fact is, however, that the original plans for a Boeing 717 family did not materialize. Only the official type designation 717-200 indicates that a shorter MD-95-20 (717-100X) as well as a stretched MD-95-50 (717-300X) had been on the drawing boards of the McDonnell Douglas and Boeing aircraft designers. They would have covered the full spectrum of the regional jet market, from 75 to 130 seats. Compared to the 717-200 that was produced, the fuselage of the "100X" model would have been shortened by four frames to 117.8 ft. (35.90 meters). Analogously, the 300X was to have been stretched by five frames to 131.9 ft. (40.20 meters). The attempt to prevent the Boeing 717 from becoming a competitor of the successful 737 was akin to a tightrope act.

The Boeing 717 prototype, registration N717XA, has since been scrapped, the only aircraft of this type to have met this fate. *Boeing Commercial Airplane Group*

This press photo released by Boeing shows one of the many possible Boeing 717 cabin layouts. In the foreground can be seen 2+2 first-class seating, and, behind it, economy class in a 2+3 seat arrangement. *Boeing Commercial Airplane Group*

Dahlewitz near Berlin, on a Boeing 717. *Boeing Commercial Airplane Group*

This image has an almost symbolic character. Sunset over the Boeing 717, of which just 156 examples were built. *Boeing Commercial Airplane Group*

The 717 development team therefore made every effort to always keep the type's range below that of the twin-engine jet from Seattle—and thus risked disinterest on the part of the airlines.

The handover of the last aircraft in May 2006 ended not only the MD-95/Boeing 717 program, but also the decades-long production of civil aircraft at Long Beach. And this was not only the beginning of the end for the tradition-rich factory in California, since nine years later, on November 29, 2015, a Boeing C-17 military transport, which had been developed by McDonnell Douglas, left the production line, becoming the last aircraft produced at Long Beach. Soon after, the plant was completely closed and torn down.

In the meantime, the Boeing 717 had become a type that was much sought after by the airlines and was extremely economical. Of the 156 jets of this type that were built, except for the prototypes, which were scrapped, all are still in service in Europe, the US, and Australia. Used 717s, when they become available, immediately find new owners—and many airline managers may regret that they did not give this aircraft program a chance when there was still time.

N717XA
BOEING 717

THE LAST DC-9S AND MD-80S WERE RETIRED EXCLUSIVELY FOR ECONOMIC REASONS. THE AIRCRAFT WERE SO EXCELLENTLY DESIGNED THAT FROM A TECHNICAL POINT OF VIEW THEY COULD STILL BE IN SERVICE TODAY.

—Nils Benker, former SAS test pilot

VG
Super 80
I-DAVG
TINENTAL

CHAPTER 2
THE DC-9 IN AIRLINE SERVICE

The following selection of buyers of brand-new and secondhand Douglas DC-9s, McDonnell Douglas MD-80s, and MD-90s, and Boeing 717 aircraft does not claim to be exhaustive. It would be beyond the scope of this book to list all the DC-9 operators since the DC-9 prototype made its first flight in 1965. Therefore, below can be found an alphabetical list of well- and lesser-known airlines that have operated the Douglas DC-9 jets—or still do.

AERO LLOYD

The DC-9 fleet operated by Aero Lloyd, which was founded at Frankfurt in 1980, consisted of up to twenty-five aircraft, including three DC-9-32s, four MD-87s, two MD-82s, and sixteen MD-83s. Aero Lloyd declared bankruptcy in October 2003 and ceased operations. After retiring the last of up to twenty-two MD-80s in 2001, the Aero Lloyd fleet consisted of a similar number of Airbus A320 and 321 jets until it ceased operations.

MD-80s of Continental Air Lines and the Italian carrier ATI on the flight line of the McDonnell Douglas factory at Long Beach in autumn 1986, just prior to delivery. *McDonnell Douglas*

The Aero Lloyd fleet was maintained in the company's maintenance hangar at Frankfurt airport. *Aero Lloyd*

AERO
AERO LLOYD
AERO LLOYD

AERO TRASPORTI ITALIANI

Founded in 1963, over the years this subsidiary of Alitalia operated up to thirty DC-9-32s and thirty-eight MD-82 jets on Italian domestic routes. In 1985, Aero Trasporti Italiani (ATI) took over Aermediterranea, another DC-9 customer. ATI, whose fleet also included ATR-42 turboprop airliners, was integrated into the parent company Alitalia in October 1994.

AIRTRAN/VALUJET

The American low-cost airline ValuJet, which starting in 1997 operated as AirTran and in 2010 was taken over by Southwest Airlines, is tied to one of the darkest chapters in the history of the DC-9. Due to incorrectly declared oxygen canisters, which were transported filled in the cargo hold contrary to regulations, one of the airline's DC-9-32s caught fire after taking off from Miami in 1996. The fire spread quickly, and within a few minutes the aircraft went out of control and crashed into the Everglades near Miami. No one on board survived the inferno.

ValuJet was operating a motley mix of secondhand DC-9-21s, DC-9-32s, and MD-80s when it acquired parent company AirTran in 1997, taking over its name after the accident for image reasons. The ValuJet brand was too burdened with the crash in the Everglades. In 1995, ValuJet had placed an order for fifty Boeing 717s, the first airline to do so, and in 1999 AirTran placed the first brand-new aircraft in service. Bought out by its low-cost competitor Southwest Airlines in 2010, AirTran was completely absorbed into its fleet in 2014, while its Boeing 717s were sold to Delta Air Lines.

ALITALIA

Alitalia, one of the most loyal of DC-9 customers, divested itself of its last member of the DC-9 family—an MD-82—in October 2012. It had received the first of forty-four DC-9 thirty-two-passenger aircraft on October 8, 1967. Two DC-9-30 freighters delivered on May 1968 supplemented the Alitalia fleet.

With ninety McDonnell Douglas MD-82s, Alitalia was among the biggest MD-80 operators worldwide. The first example of this type, bearing the registration I-DAWA, was received in December 1983.

AUSTRIAN AIRLINES

Founded on September 30, 1957, Austrian Airlines (AUA) began flight operations with four Vickers Viscount 779s leased from Fred Olsen Lines A/S of Norway at the beginning of the summer season in 1958. The year 1960 saw the addition of the first of six of its own Vickers Viscount 837s, and three years later the airline entered the jet age with the SE 210 Caravelle VI-R. Nine brand-new DC-9-32s were delivered in 1971–72, replacing the Viscount turboprops and the comparatively uneconomical SE 210 Caravelles on AUA's European route network. Six larger DC-9-51s followed in 1975, and in October 1977, AUA's supervisory board decided to acquire eight DC-9-81s, the first of which entered service on October 26, 1980. Thirteen McDonnell Douglas MD-82s, three MD-83s, and five MD-87s completed the airline's fleet of aircraft produced at Long Beach, California, until in cooperation with Swissair, AUA selected the Airbus A320 family as its follow-on type.

One of ATI's DC-9-32s in flight over the crater of the Sicilian volcano Mount Etna. *ATI*

This Delta Air Lines Boeing 717-200 with the fleet number 9587 marked on its tail had previously been operated by Bangkok Airways, Spanair, and Blue1 before being delivered to Delta in 2016. *Delta Air Lines*

ValuJet, which in 1997 began operating under the name AirTran, placed firm orders for fifty McDonnell Douglas MD-95s and options on fifty more in 1995. *Boeing Commercial Airplane Group*

The DC-9-32 formed the backbone of Alitalia's European traffic in the 1960s and 1970s. The DC-9-32 shown here with the registration I-DIKC was delivered new from Douglas in December 1967 and given the name Isola die Ponza by Alitalia.

The DC-9-33AF cargo version was capable of carrying a payload of 34,171 lbs. (15.5 metric tons) over a range of 1,180 miles (1,900 kilometers). *SAS*

In the 1970s, a DC-9-41 takes off against the imposing rocky backdrop of the Svalbard archipelago. Its airport, Longyearbyen, is the most northerly airport in the world with regular airline service. *SAS*

A McDonnell Douglas DC-9-81 overflies the snow-capped peaks of the Austrian Alps. Swissair and Austrian were the first customers for this variant of the DC-9. *AUA*

Presentation of the shuttle service jointly offered by Austrian Airlines and Swissair in 1995. *ETH-Bibliothek Zurich, Swissair*

The MD-80s of Austrian Airlines and Swissair, which shuttled between Vienna and Zurich, were given a special livery in the 1990s as part of the joint-venture flights. *ETH-Bibliothek Zurich, Swissair*

ATLANTIS

Based in Frankfurt, in the late 1960s to early 1970s the German charter airline Atlantis was, like Pan International, Air Commerz, and Aviaction, one of the depreciation companies common at the time, whose loss allocations helped wealthy shareholders legally reduce their high tax burdens. The airline flew its three DC-9-32s from West German airports to warm-water destinations around the Mediterranean, and three brand-new DC-8-63CF long-range jets on charter routes to North America. The airline, launched in 1968, was forced to suspend operations in October 1982 as a result of economic difficulties.

BALAIR AND BALAIR CTA

For decades, Balair and Balair CTA were the charter divisions of the Swiss airline Swissair. Under the name Balair, the airline maintained routes on behalf of Swissair flying Fokker F-27s (for example, from Zurich to Innsbruck) and transported people and materiel to crisis regions of the world for the International Red Cross. In addition to the F-27, DC-6s, DC-8-63s, and DC-10-30s also flew in the livery of Balair, which also rented additional Swissair capacity as needed. After the merger with CTA, based in Geneva in 1993, the MD-82, -83, and -87 fleets of both airlines and Airbus A310-300 long-range jets operated together on charter routes. After Swissair became insolvent, in autumn 2001 Balair CTA was also forced to cease operations.

BLUE1

In 1998, Scandinavian Airlines acquired the Finnish regional airline Air Botnia, which had found itself in financial difficulties, then restructured the company and henceforth used it as a regional feeder for its European route network and on Finnish domestic routes from Helsinki. In 2004, the airline became Blue1, and, with its BAE 146s and RJ100 Regional Jets, took on new tasks for SAS. After they were retired by SAS, up to five MD-90-30s were flown for a time by Blue1, whose fleet was standardized in 2010 with nine Boeing 717s. Each of these aircraft was painted in an individual color scheme designed by Finnish design students. Blue1 divested itself of its last Boeing 717 in November 2015, bringing to an end the "DC-9 era" in the SAS group. As had been the case with the airline's five MD-90s, Delta Air Lines also acquired Blue1's nine Boeing 717s.

BRITISH MIDLAND

Based at Castle Donington, starting in 1976 British Midland (BMI) operated a mix of DC-9-14s, -15s, and -32s, purchased secondhand or leased, on British domestic routes and its European route network. The DC-9s were used to expand the airline and replace its dated Vickers Viscount turboprops. Following an interlude with Lufthansa, since 2012 BMI, whose roots go back to 1938, has been part of the International Airlines Group (IAG) and has become part of British Airways.

The German vacation airline Atlantic took delivery of Schwabenland, a DC-9-32 with the registration D-ADIS, brand new in January 1970. After the airline went bankrupt, in 1973 the aircraft was sold to North Central Airline in the United States, before the former Schwabenland became part of the second-largest DC-9 fleet in the world following North Central's merger with Republic Airlines and its takeover by Northwest Airlines. *Atlantis*

This MD-82 flew for Balair between 1993 and 1995 with the registration HB-INB. *ETH-Bibliothek Zurich, Swissair*

Two of Balair CTA's MD-80s being serviced at Swissair's maintenance base.
ETH-Bibliothek Zurich, Swissair

Blue
Blue1

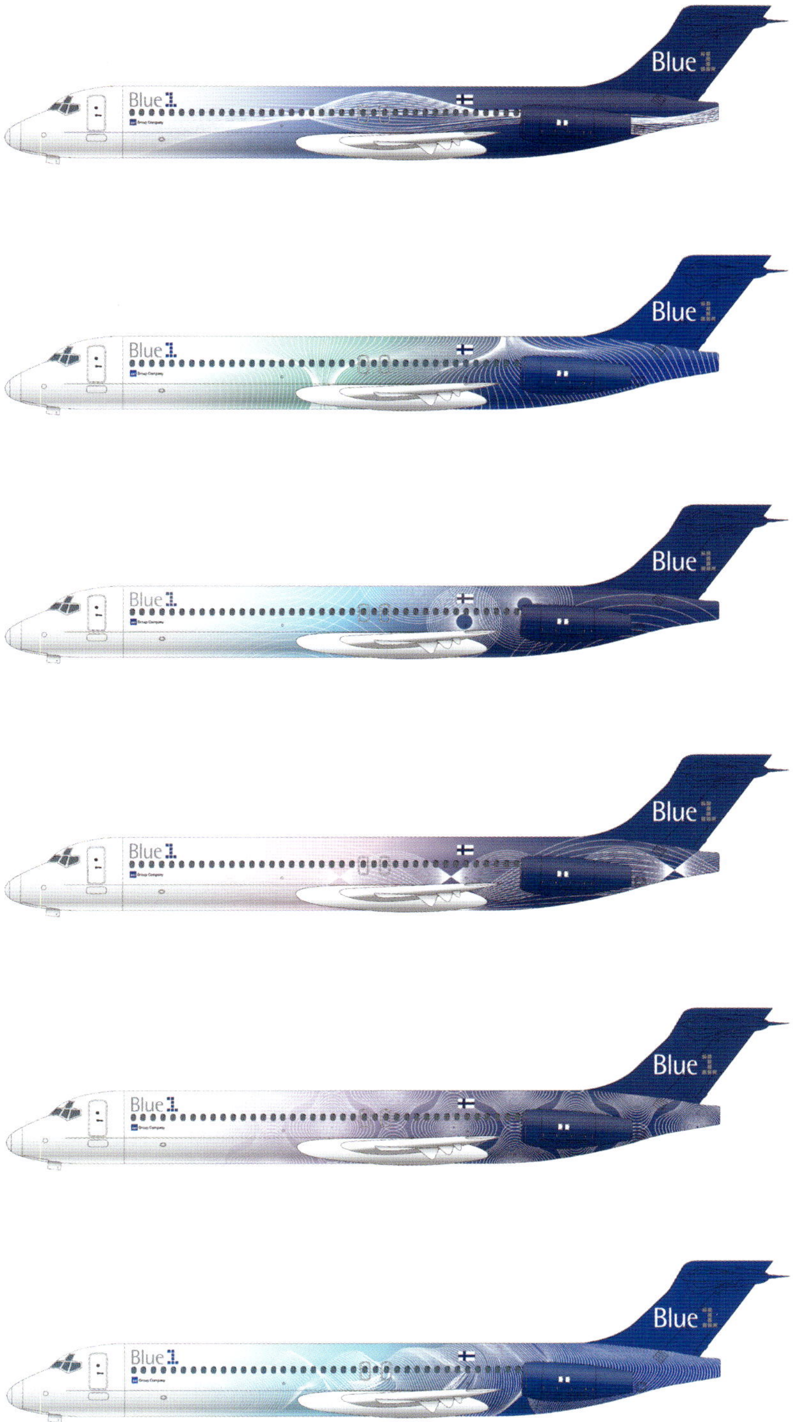

A McDonnell Douglas MD-90-30 of Blue1 about to touch down at its home airfield of Helsinki-Vantaa. *Blue1*

Six of the nine different Blue1 Boeing 717 livery variations. *Blue1*

BM
British Midland BM
G-BMAM
The Cullinan Diamond

CROSSAIR

Based in Basel, until 1995 the Swiss regional airline Crossair operated up to twelve MD-80s on its charter and scheduled routes—including on behalf of Swissair. The MD-82s operated by Crossair had 149 seats, while its MD-83s had a 161-seat configuration. When the SAS Group, which included Swissair, declared bankruptcy in October 2001, the present-day SWISS International Airlines, which since 2005 has been a 100 percent subsidiary of the Lufthansa Group, was created on the basis of Crossair.

DELTA AIR LINES

Delta Air Lines was the first customer for the DC-9-10, which entered service on November 29, 1965, and the largest airline in the world has remained loyal to this type of aircraft in a special way. With 110 MD-88s, sixty-four MD-90s, and ninety-one Boeing 717s, in autumn 2017 it had the largest fleet of these three DC-9 derivatives anywhere in the world. Delta's enthusiasm for this type was shared by Northwest Airlines, which merged with it in 2008, adding its large DC-9 fleet to that of Delta. Over the years, 197 DC-9s of most versions—except for the Series 21—have flown in Northwest's striking livery. Some of these dated aircraft initially remained in service after the merger with Delta. Not until January 2014 was Delta finally able to divest itself of its last six remaining DC-9s. Fittingly, the final flight was from Northwest Orient's former home base of Minneapolis–St. Paul to Delta's corporate headquarters in Atlanta, Georgia. The DC-9 era was far from over for Delta, however, since the best replacement for a DC-9—is a DC-9. And so the last DC-9 classics were replaced by aircraft of the MD-95 / Boeing 717 replacement generation. Hardly distinguishable externally by most passengers, in this way the Douglas story will live on for a while to come in the last civil aircraft developed and produced by McDonnell Douglas and Boeing at Long Beach.

FINNAIR

Finnair is among the oldest Douglas customers and placed its first DC-2 in service in 1941. With its twenty-seven Series 10, 40, and 50 DC-9s, from 1971 Finnair served a dense route network inside Finland and in eastern and western Europe. Some of the aircraft were purchased new from Douglas, while others were acquired secondhand from other airlines. This included part of the DC-9-10 fleet and all six of the airline's DC-9-40s, which were procured from TOA Domestic of Japan.

The DC-9 classics were replaced by twenty-six Series 82, 83, and 87 MD-80s, which also operated on scheduled and charter services from Helsinki before having to give way to more-modern Airbus jets of the A320 family and Boeing 757s.

In addition to its DC-9-32s (*left*), over the decades British Midland, the second-largest British airline, also flew DC-9-14s and -15s. In the 1980s and 1990s the airline's entire DC-9 fleet was replaced by modern Boeing 737-300s, -400s, and -500s. *British Midland*

Crossair advertising leaflet for a flight on its MD-82/-83. *Crossair*

For a time, a Crossair MD-83 flew in this striking livery as the "McPlane," advertising for the fast-food chain and the Swiss tour operator Hotelplan. *Crossair*

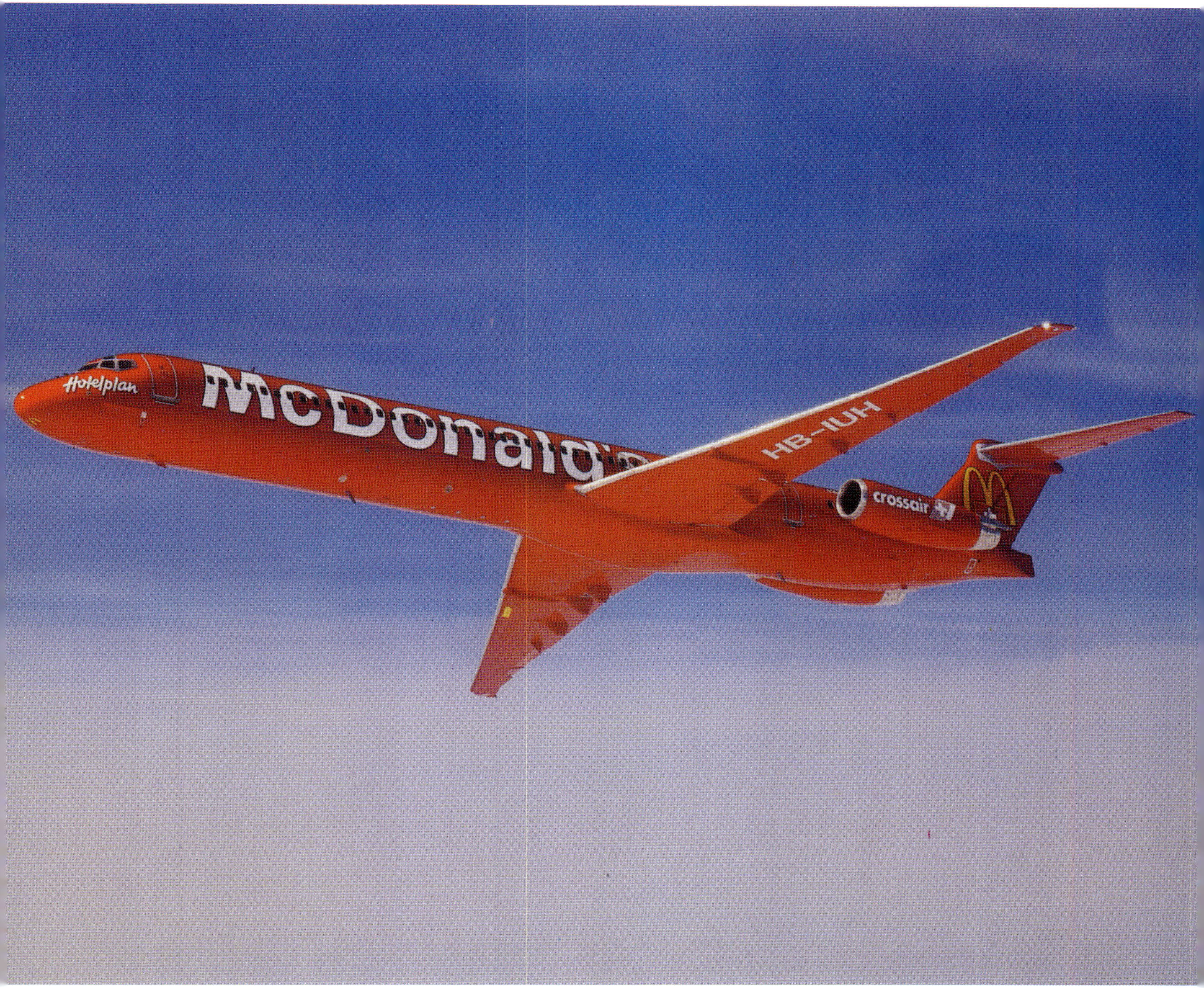
Hotelplan
McDonald's
HB-IUH
crossair

An MD-82 in the airline's standard livery over the peaks of the Swiss Alps. *Crossair*

DELTA
N903DA
DELTA

MD-90 taking off from its home base at Atlanta. *Delta Air Lines*

This Delta Air Lines advertising leaflet depicts the stars of its fleet in the 1970s: top to bottom, Douglas DC-9-32, Boeing 727-200, and Lockheed L-1011. *Delta Air Lines*

In the 1980s, American artist Mike Machat designed this motif of Finnair's fleet history for the airline—from the Junkers F-13 of the 1920s to the Douglas DC-10-30. *Finnair*

FINNAIR
FINNAIR
FINNAIR

FINNAIR

The prominent tail of a Finnair DC-9. *Finnair*

Even the meeting of the airline's DC-3 Dakota tradition aircraft with its McDonnell Douglas / Boeing descendant was not enough to move the airline to purchase the MD-95/717. While more than 10,600 examples of the legendary DC-3 were built, just 156 Boeing 717s were completed. *Boeing Commercial Airplane Group*

GREAT AMERICAN AIRWAYS

This American airline began operations on September 26, 1979—initially with a single DC-9-15. The small fleet quickly grew to three aircraft of the same type. Great American Airways' main business was transporting gamers to the numerous casinos in the Reno, Nevada, region. In 1994 the airline procured an MD-87 from SAZ Airline of Egypt, followed by a second MD-87 and an MD-82 just a year later. In 1996, Great American wet-leased two MD-83s to Air Jamaica, operating them on Caribbean routes under its name.

Following the crash of a ValuJet DC-9, in the first quarter of 1997 the American regulatory agency, the FAA, also closely scrutinized Great American Airways' safety standards. The result was so devastating that on April 13, 1997, the FAA immediately grounded the airline. As a direct consequence of the grounding, Great American filed for bankruptcy protection under Chapter 11 of the US Bankruptcy Code just one day later. The company was not to resume operations again.

This aircraft's livery reveals that Trans World Airlines (TWA) was the previous owner of the DC-9-15. Originally delivered brand new from Douglas to TWA on May 30, 1967, in August 1979, Great American Airways became the Douglas jet's second owner. *Great American*

HUGHES AIRWEST

On August 12, 1968, Nick Bez, chairman of the board of the American airline Air West, announced the sale of the company to airline tycoon Howard Hughes. This occurred just four months after Air West, based in San Francisco, was formed by the merger of the airlines Bonanza, Pacific, and West Coast. Bonanza and West Coast were already using DC-9s; therefore Air West and subsequently Hughes Airwest also remained true to this type. Howard Hughes, who had lost his share in TWA after an internal power struggle, took a 78 percent stake through Hughes Tool Company, which he controlled, and the remaining 22 percent directly in Air West, which was renamed Hughes Airwest in March 1970, just one day after the deal was finally settled. As the company's name suggests, with its fleet of DC-9-10s and -32s, Hughes Airwest, based at the San Francisco airport, served mainly destinations on the West Coast of the US, Mexico, and Canada. The company, which lasted just ten years, came to an end on October 1, 1980, four years after the death of Howard Hughes, when it was taken over by Republic Airlines—which in turn became part of Delta Air Lines in 2009 in the American takeover merry-go-round.

Refueling a DC-9-32 of Hughes Airwest, which operated on the American West Coast from 1970 to 1980. As its name suggests, the airline was founded by the aviator and airline tycoon Howard Hughes.

IBERIA

Founded in 1927 with financial support from Lufthansa, the Sociedad Ibérica de Aviación (Iberia) was one of the largest customers for the DC-9 family of airliners, acquiring fifty DC-9-30s, fourteen MD-88s, one MD-83, and twenty-four MD-87s. The first DC-9 became part of the Iberia fleet on June 30, 1967, and the airline used the reliable twin-engine jets on its extended European route network. After the last MD-80s were retired, aircraft of the Airbus A320 series took over their role in European air traffic.

KLM

Founded on October 7, 1919, KLM, the oldest airline in the world still operating under its original company name, was a faithful Douglas customer for many decades. KLM ordered every type from Long Beach, beginning with the DC-2; continuing through the DC-3 Dakota, DC-4, DC-6, DC-7, DC-8, DC-9, and DC-10; to the MD-11. Even the DC-5, which was produced only in small numbers, flew in the colors of Royal Dutch Airlines.

KLM was one of the first airlines to order the new jet from Long Beach, California. The DC-9-15 "City of Amsterdam," delivered on March 25, 1966, was followed by five more aircraft of the same type. Starting in November 1967, KLM expanded its fleet, adding thirteen examples of the larger DC-9-32, while six DC-9-33RC (Rapid Change) also entered service with the Flying Dutchmen in 1968–69. Equipped with a side cargo door on the main deck, this version could be converted from a pure passenger version to a freighter in a very short time.

KLM was one of Douglas's most loyal customers for more than seven decades. Despite this, unlike other longtime Douglas customers it did not select the MD-80 and MD-90 to succeed its DC-9 classics, instead choosing the Boeing 737-300 and -400 family of aircraft, the first time it had opted for a product from a competitor of its traditional aircraft provider.

OZARK AIRLINES

Founded in 1950 and taken over by Trans World Airlines (TWA) in 1986, in January 1965 Ozark Airlines announced that it planned to take off into the future with the DC-9-15. This initial order was followed in the same year by an order for DC-9-31s. For a time, the Ozark DC-9 fleet numbered fifty aircraft, and in addition to the DC-9-15 and -31 the company, based at St. Louis, also flew examples of the -41 and MD-82 versions.

This photo of a model of a McDonnell Douglas MD-87 published by Iberia announced the entry into service of twenty-four aircraft of this type with the Spanish national airline in 1990 and 1991. *Iberia*

Although KLM was a loyal Douglas customer for decades, the Dutch airline selected the Boeing 737-300 from Douglas's competitor Boeing to replace its fleet of DC-9-30s. *ETH-Bibliothek Zurich, Swissair*

A DC-9-32 of the American airline Ozark Air Lines, which in 1986 merged with TWA. The aircraft illustrated here was originally delivered to Delta Air Lines in 1967 and ten years later became part of the Ozark fleet. The airline's advertising slogan: "The OZARK DC-9 by McDonnell Douglas . . . We make it easy for you." *Ozark Air Lines*

QUANTASLINK

Founded in 1992, Impulse Airlines of Australia initially flew on regional routes until 2000, when it acquired Boeing 717s and repositioned itself as a low-cost carrier. It was acquired by Quantas in November 2001, after which its Boeing 717s operated on the QuantasLink network. Impulse officially ceased operations in 2004, and in the summer of 2022 National Jet Systems operated a fleet of Boeing 717s on behalf of QuantasLink.

SCANDINAVIAN AIRLINES SYSTEM

With nine DC-9-21s, two DC-9-33AF freighters, and forty-nine DC-9-41s, at the end of the 1970s Scandinavian Airlines System (SAS) had one of the largest DC-9 fleets outside the United States. McDonnell Douglas developed the DC-9-21 and -41 specifically for the Flying Vikings' route network. In the 1980s SAS was one of the first customers for the DC-9-81 and the MD-81, -82, -83, and -87 variants, some of which it retrofitted with glass cockpits itself.

For a time, DC-9-32s and -51s leased from Swissair and Inex Adria also flew in the colors of the trinational airline of Sweden, Norway, and Denmark, and thus every version of the classic DC-9 saw service with SAS except the DC-9-10 base model. After the airline had ordered the further-stretched MD-90-30, an order for the MD-95 to replace its older DC-9s seemed certain. But things were to turn out differently, and SAS chose the Boeing 737-600 instead. For McDonnell Douglas this not only meant the bitter loss of a large contract thought to be secure, but also served as the warning signal for other potential MD-95 customers, who henceforth gave preference to the Boeing product and thus spurred the end of the MD-95 / Boeing 717 program. Disappointed by the high operating costs of its Boeing jets, years later SAS decided to purchase secondhand MD-95 / Boeing 717s. As many as nine examples were operated, not in its own fleet but by its Spanish and Finnish subsidiaries Spanair and Blue1. It was not until 2016 that Blue1's aircraft were replaced by Bombardier CRJ 900 Regional Jets. The last DC-9 left the SAS fleet in 2001, followed by the MD-90 in 2012. A large celebration was held to mark the retirement of the last MD-80 in 2013.

SPANAIR

Founded in 1986, the Spanish airline Spanair was an associate company of SAS. It offered both charter flights and scheduled connections between Spanish, other European, and intercontinental destinations. Spanair was also a member of Star Alliance, which SAS helped found in 1997. The airline operated MD-82s, -83s, and -87s (some leased from SAS), Boeing 717s, and Airbus A320 and A321 jets on its European routes. For a time, it also operated Boeing 767-300ERs on long-range routes to North and South America. In 2012, Spanair was forced to cease operations because of financial difficulties, in part because of the crash of one of its MD-80s four years earlier, and went bankrupt.

Cobham Airline Services of Australia began operating eight Boeing 717s on behalf of QuantasLink in autumn 2017. Another twelve aircraft of this type were operated by National Jet Systems. The aircraft seen here, registration VH-YQS, was part of the Cobham fleet. *Quantas*

Two DC-9-33AF freighters flew for SAS and in the 1980s for Air de Cologne, which it founded as an express freight company based at Cologne/Bonn airport. *SAS*

Servicing an SAS MD-87 at its major hub—the airport of the Danish capital, Copenhagen. *SAS*

This DC-9-81, named "Maria Viking" and registered SE-DMZ, was originally delivered to Swissair with the registration HB-INK and the aircraft name "Opfikon." *SAS*

A Spanair MD-83 during a technical check at the Swissair maintenance facility at Zurich-Kloten airport. *ETH-Bibliothek Zurich, Swissair*

SWISSAIR

The Swiss airline received its first DC-9s in 1966–67, adding five Series 15 aircraft to its fleet. These were followed by the larger DC-9-32 and -33 freighters, before Swissair initiated two bestselling variants of the DC-9 with the DC-9-51 and -81. Because of its close cooperation with SAS, Swissair DC-9s sometimes flew in the colors of the Scandinavian airline, while SAS DC-9-41s operated on the Swiss airline's route network.

Swissair was the first customer for the DC-9-51, with an order for twelve aircraft, and together with Austrian Airlines it was also the launch customer for the DC-9-81, from which the MD-81 was developed. While Swissair placed the first DC-9-51 in service on August 24, 1975, the first of an initial order for fifteen DC-9-81s followed in October 1980. After further orders, Swissair's fleet of MD-81s ultimately reached twenty-five aircraft, of which two were converted into the MD-82 version and three into MD-83s. Swissair also leased an MD-82 from its charter subsidiary Balair between 1993 and 1995. Beginning in 1995, the airline's MD-80 fleet was gradually replaced by Airbus A319s, A320s, and A321s.

Swissair operated a DC-9-33F on its European cargo routes between 1969 and 1984. *ETH-Bibliothek Zurich, Swissair*

Swissair was the launch customer for the DC-9-81. *ETH-Bibliothek Zurich, Swissair*

THY: TURK HAVA YOLLARI

THY ordered ten examples of the DC-9-32 on July 9, 1968, and these aircraft were operated on domestic routes and to European destinations. At times, several of these DC-9-32s flew in the colors of THY's Turkish Cypriot subsidiary Kibris Hava Yollari. In the 1970s, THY's European fleet also included Fokker F-28s and Boeing 727-200 jets.

VOLOTEA

Volotea, a Spanish low-cost airline founded in 2011, began operations in 2012. At the time this book was being written, its fleet consisted mainly of seventeen Boeing 717s in a 125-seat configuration in addition to Airbus A319 aircraft. Following the retirement of Blue1's last aircraft in 2015, in autumn 2017 it was the only European airline still operating this aircraft type. In the summer of 2022 Volotea had grounded her remaining 727s—possibly for good.

The Douglas DC-9-32s of Turk Hava Yollari and the airline's Boeing 727-200s were frequent visitors to German airports in the 1970s. *THY*

When this book went to print, the Spanish airline Volotea still had four 717s in the fleet, which were taken out of service and placed in storage.

MY IDEA FOR EASY-TO-USE ONBOARD PASSENGER STAIRS FOR THE 737 WAS WELL RECEIVED BY BOEING—AND THAT IS EXACTLY WHAT WAS BUILT ON THE PRODUCTION LINE!

—Professor Ernst Simon, longtime head of the Lufthansa Technical Projects Department

BOEING 737-600
737
737
N737BX

CHAPTER 3
THE COMPETITORS

When the DC-9 was launched, both of its direct competitors were produced in Europe. Development of the Boeing 737, which has since passed the DC-9 as the most-produced jet aircraft, began two years after the DC-9.

When the Douglas Aircraft Company began concrete planning for its new twin-jet in 1963, there were only two competing designs in the Western world also powered by two turbojet engines: the French SE 210 Caravelle and the British BAC 111. Even by the time of the Douglas DC-9's maiden flight in 1965, this situation had not changed.

The Boeing 737, whose prototype flew for the first time in 1967, did not enter the competition for orders until two years after Douglas. By the beginning of the 1970s, it had become obvious that the European types, which were no longer state of the art, had to concede defeat to their American competitors, the DC-9 and Boeing 737. The last SE 210 left the final production line in Toulouse in 1972, while the last of just 235 BAC 111s produced in Great Britain was completed in June 1984.

Previous pages: Like Douglas with its DC-9, Boeing also offered a family of aircraft to meet the different requirements of its customers. Here, in formation flight, the 737 next-generation types Boeing 737-700 (*left*), 737-800 (*below*), and 737-600. Scandinavian airline SAS selected the latter in place of the MD-95, which almost led to the complete cessation of the alternative McDonnell Douglas program. *Boeing*

An SAS SE 210 at Oslo-Fornebu airport. *SAS*

SAS
SE-DAB
SCANDINAVIAN AIRLINES SYSTEM

SE 210 CARAVELLE

If the aircraft construction adage "If it looks right, it flies right" ever applied to an aircraft type, than it was the French Caravelle. Its design was something of a technical revolution in aircraft construction. The first jet specially designed for short and medium ranges was novel in having two engines arranged in the tail. This design feature, later adopted by the BAC 111, Douglas DC-9, and Tupolev Tu 134, limited noise in the passenger cabin to the rear rows of seats. This made a trip aboard the SE 210 a very comfortable experience for most passengers. It is no wonder that the Caravelle was very popular with air travelers.

The pilots who had the privilege to fly the SE 210 were as enthusiastic as the type's passengers. With what other jet airliner could one circle like a glider in the thermals beneath the clouds with the two Rolls-Royce Avon engines at idle?

The SE 210 was the result of a national French competition, in which the aircraft manufacturers Bréguet / SNCA du Nord, Hurel-Dubois, SNCA du Sud-Ouest, and SNCA du Sud-Est took part with their jet designs. The nose section of the SE 210 was notable in that it was identical to that of the de Havilland DH 106 Comet. Although no other Comet design features were adopted, the British manufacturer provided the details for the design of the French type's distinctive forward fuselage.

Initially conceived as a three-engine aircraft powered by French SNECMA Atar E3 engines, at the request of the selection committee, Sud-Est changed it to a twin-engine aircraft with more-powerful Rolls-Royce RA 16 Avon engines. This concept was presented to the French secretary for civil aviation (SGACC) for examination in July 1952. The design appeared to have convinced the authorities straightaway, since just two months later the Société Nationale de Construction Aéronautique du Sud-Est Aviation (SNCASE), Sud-Est Aviation for short, was awarded the contract. Work on two flying prototypes began in February 1953. There was also a fuselage for structural-fatigue tests in a water tank, as well as static tests. Prior to the issuing of the final contract on July 2, 1953, the project lost its experimental designation and henceforth officially became the SE 210.

France's national airline, Air France, placed an initial order for twelve aircraft and at the same time secured twelve options, but then, however, the order books in Toulouse initially remained empty. Although the Caravelle had gained international attention, no airline could bring itself to order the technologically revolutionary jet airliner. In addition to the key question of the economic viability of the then-novel jet propulsion over short- and medium-distance routes, the numerous innovative design details caused mistrust—the SE 210 Caravelle was the first jet whose control surfaces all were hydraulically operated. The use of industrial adhesives was revived, and these were employed widely to reduce weight, as had been done on the Comet. And finally, Sud-Est Aviation was a blank canvas in civil aircraft construction, whose salespeople also had to struggle with language problems. Almost no one in the company spoke English at that time—and conversely, knowledge of French was limited among the airlines that might purchase the aircraft. And so, the Caravelle's story would have been a short one had not the Scandinavian airline SAS taken a liking to the elegant machine from the south of France.

The enthusiasm of the Danes, Norwegians, and Swedes permeated the entire company and was not limited to the airline's board of directors. Instead, the appearance of the elegant jet, which Sud-Est Aviation sent on several demonstrations to the Far North, caused an outbreak of "Caravelle fever" among the otherwise rather cool Scandinavians. A pub called the Caravelle Inn opened at Copenhagen-Kastrup airport just for passengers on the demonstration flights. The song "Caravelle Samba," commissioned by SAS, celebrated the elegant jet with the words "Voici la Caravelle . . . she's really something swell." Wherever SAS opened a route with the elegant jet, the local papers were filled with euphoric reports. On many press flights, journalists also had the opportunity to gain a personal impression of flying on the innovative short-and-medium-range jet. Most accounts effusively extolled the aircraft's elegance, its comfort, and the speed bestowed by the new jet engines—precisely as the SAS PR department had hoped.

On May 25, 1957, the SAS board of directors made the formal decision to initially purchase six SE 210 Caravelles. This contract had a certain prestige value, because after their pioneering development of polar air traffic in the 1950s, the Scandinavians were considered trendsetters in the commercial aviation field. Before long, Alitalia, Finnair, and Varig of Brazil had also ordered the new jetliner from Toulouse.

The first SE 210 Caravelle I for SAS, with the construction number 03, arrived at Stockholm-Bromma on April 13, 1959. A few days later, on April 26, the "Finn Viking" took off on its first commercial flight from Copenhagen to Beirut. Thus, even before Air France, SAS had the honor of using a Caravelle on a scheduled service for the first time anywhere in the world. Perhaps this was the French way of thanking SAS management, without whose farsightedness this revolutionary design would probably have been denied commercial success.

With up to forty-six aircraft, Air France not only maintained the largest Caravelle fleet but also used the type longer than any other early customer. The last SE 210 did not leave the Air France fleet until 1981—after more than two decades of service.

The SE 210 I, IA, and III versions were followed by the Caravelle VI-N with two Rolls-Royce Mk. 531 Avon engines. The first customer was United Airlines, which on February 25, 1960, ordered twenty of the VI-R version, the first with thrust reversal. Thrust reversal rendered the braking parachute used by earlier versions of the SE 210 for landings on short and wet runways superfluous. In response to a requirement by the FAA, the aircraft for United were fitted with larger cockpit windows to give the pilots a better all-around view. They subsequently became standard on all later variants of the SE 210.

After Trans World Airlines (TWA) placed an order for twenty Caravelle VIIs in September 1960, Sud Aviation hoped for a breakthrough into the American market. They were to be powered by General Electric CJ805-23C turbofan engines, based on those used by the Convair CV 990 Coronado. After TWA canceled the order for economic reasons, Sud Aviation offered the engine as equipment for the Caravelle 10A, which aroused little enthusiasm on the part of any airline.

More successful was the SE 210 10B version, with Pratt & Whitney JT8D-1 turbofan engines, then regarded as the industry standard, which also powered the first Boeing 737s and Douglas DC-9s. The Caravelle 10B and 10R models, with more-powerful JT8D-7 engines, and the 11R combi (airliner/freighter) version finally prepared the way for the ultimate Caravelle variants. The Danish charter airline Sterling was the first customer for this Caravelle 12, whose fuselage was stretched more than 19.7 ft. (6 meters) compared to the basic model. Powered by two JT8D-9 engines, the Caravelle 12 could accommodate 140 passengers with charter seating. Production of the SE 210 ended in 1972 after the delivery of five more Super Douze (Super Twelve) aircraft to the French domestic carrier Air Inter, after a total of 282 aircraft had been built.

The Belgian airline Sabena operated two leased BAC-111s and its own Boeing 737-200s in the 1990s. *Sabena*

BRITISH AIRCRAFT CORPORATION (BAC 111)

The design of the BAC 111 was derived from a project study by Hunting Aircraft Limited with the designation H-107 in the 1950s; however, it was the merger of the British aviation industry into the British Aircraft Corporation (BAC) at the beginning of the 1960s that provided the final impetus for production of this twin jet. The BAC 111 prototype with the registration G-ASHG left the final assembly building at Hurn on July 28, 1963, and it made its first flight just a few weeks later on August 20. The One Eleven was powered by two Rolls-Royce Spey turbojets of various versions and thrust ratings. In the 1960s, the Spey was the standard power plant for British short- and medium-range jets, and in addition to the BAC 111 it also powered the Hawker Siddeley HS 121 Trident.

British United Airways, the BAC 111 launch customer, took delivery of its first aircraft on January 22, 1965. Even before the One Eleven's first flight, three American operators—American Airlines, Braniff, and Mohawk Airlines—ordered significant numbers of the British jet. During the 1960s, BAC developed a number of versions of the BAC 111, and the stretched 500 version attracted the interest of British European Airways (BEA). The manufacturer had high hopes for continued sales success and opened a second final-assembly line in Weybridge. In fact, not only was the One Eleven a great hope of the British aviation industry, but with 244 aircraft produced in Great Britain and Romania, it was built in greater numbers than any other first-generation British civilian jet.

In Germany, the BAC 111 was very popular with the charter airlines. Bavaria and Germanair, which merged in 1977 and from which Hapag-Lloyd Flug emerged as the predecessor of the present-day TUI Fly two years later, were particularly fond of the British medium-range jet's economy of operation. This differed from Lufthansa, which resisted strong internal political pressure and refused to purchase the European product, instead deciding in 1965 on the Boeing 737, then a completely newly conceived short-and-medium-range jet.

sabena
OO-SDO

The BAC 111's greatest shortcoming was its very loud turbojet engines. The jacket of cooler air produced by a modern turbofan engine, which seals in the noise at its source, was absent from the One Eleven. BAC did develop hush kits, which could be fitted retroactively, to reduce noise, but their effect was marginal. As a result, all BAC 111s commercially licensed in Europe had to be decommissioned by April 1, 2002, at the latest, since they failed to meet the strict Chapter 3 noise limits imposed by JAA, the then European airspace authority. A sound damper presented jointly by the British airline European Aviation and the American company Quiet Technology made the BAC 111 into a Chapter 3 aircraft; however, it was never approved for the larger BAC 111 Series 500 used on scheduled services. The system was fitted to only five converted business jets of the smaller 400 series, which were approved in the United States. More promising, however, was the more radical concept from the American Dee Howard Inc. As early as 1990, it planned to reequip BAC 111 business jets with even-quieter and more-fuel-efficient Rolls-Royce Tay Mk. 650 turbofan engines. There was little customer interest, however, and just two examples of the BAC 111 2400 were built for demonstration purposes.

While new and improved versions of the competing Boeing 737 and Douglas DC-9 designs were sold in large numbers, production of the BAC 111, built in Great Britain, came to an end on June 6, 1984, after 235 examples had been built.

This was not quite the end of the One Eleven, however, since in Romania the state-owned aircraft maker CNIAR produced the ROMBAC 111 under license. This ambitious joint venture initially planned to produce as many as eighty aircraft, but there was little interest in the project, and just nine aircraft were completed. The last aircraft, with the registration YR-BRI, was delivered to the Romanian state airline Romavia in 1991.

Of the 244 BAC 111s that were built, just two examples were still flying in 2017, used by Northrop Grumman in the United States as avionics and electronic test bed aircraft. When these two aircraft, registered N162W and N164W, are retired in the foreseeable future, the chapter of the last jet airliner completely built in Great Britain and powered by British engines will finally come to an end.

BOEING 737

When Boeing began project studies for a small twin-engine jet on May 8, 1964, the competition had long since positioned itself in the market with its own designs. The French Sud Aviation SE 210 Caravelle had been flying in scheduled service since 1958, and British Aircraft Corporation unveiled its BAC 111 in 1961, while that same year, archrival Douglas in Long Beach, California, presented its Model 2086, which became the DC-9, officially launched in April 1963. The concept initially pursued by Boeing mirrored the designs of the other producers and envisaged a small jet with a narrow fuselage and two engines in the tail.

If Boeing wanted to offer an economical airliner with a two-man cockpit, its maximum takeoff weight had to be under 80,000 pounds (36.3 metric tons). This was the upper limit, introduced on March 31, 1949, at the insistence of the American Pilots Association (ALPA), above which commercial aircraft registered in the US had to be equipped with a three-man cockpit. Heavier jets were also to be flown by three pilots, not two pilots and one flight engineer—because ALPA raised safety concerns, and, according to contemporary witnesses, stood up to the rival Association of Flight Engineers. These were the conditions that the 737 development team of Joe Sutter, Dave Norton, and Jack E. Steiner faced when they began detailed work on the design of the new jet.

Still undecided about the configuration of the new jet, Boeing's marketing department was already pushing for a jet that was even smaller than the DC-9. This was to avoid competing with the larger Boeing 727 and to attract customers for smaller jets to Boeing. Only joint studies between Boeing and United Airlines in the summer of 1964 gave preference to a cabin cross section that corresponded in its dimensions to the forward fuselage of a 727.

From July 12 to 17 of that year, 737 program manager Jack Steiner and Joe Sutter visited Lufthansa's technical base in Hamburg. Although Gerhard Höltje, Lufthansa's chief technical officer, was relatively sympathetic to the Boeing design, Lufthansa's headquarters in Cologne at that time still favored the Douglas DC-9. The small Boeing jet, with its engines located in the tail, was reminiscent in its basic features of the HFB Hansa Jet, which was being built south of the Elbe in Hamburg-Finkenwerder at the time, and which took off on its maiden flight on April 21, 1964. Sutter and Steiner therefore took the opportunity to meet with the Hamburger Flugzeugbau GmbH designers and test pilots to discuss the advantages and disadvantages of a T tail and tail-mounted engines. The HFB team willingly presented the aerodynamic wind tunnel data for the Hansa Jet, which surprised Steiner and Sutter. They had not reckoned that the danger of a "locked-in stall" (that is, the complete loss of control over the aircraft at a high angle of attack) would be so dramatic with a T tail. What could happen was tragically demonstrated about a year later during Hansa Jet flight tests near Madrid. The HFB320 prototype crashed as a result of a deliberate stall during the certification flights, and despite all the precautions taken beforehand, test pilot Loren "Swede" Davis was killed.

On their return to Seattle, Sutter and Steiner focused on two possible design variants, each powered by two Pratt & Whitney JTF-10 engines. The goal remained a small jet, well below the seating capacity of the Boeing 727-100 and the Douglas DC-9. The only question was whether a T tail with tail-mounted engines or a solution with engines mounted in nacelles under the wings was the better variant.

Two groups, led by Erik Lund and Peyton Autry, now looked into the two alternatives. While both had their offices in the 727 development center, the two were supposed to have as little contact with each other as possible in order to achieve the best independent results. This competition lasted several months and involved numerous wind tunnel tests. The main focus was not the economic viability of the two alternatives, which Jack Steiner judged to be equal, but instead operational advantages and disadvantages. The jet was still supposed to be smaller than the Douglas DC-9, which led to a design that, due to its extremely wide fuselage taken from the 727, reminded some of a bumblebee. Soon the Boeing offices in Seattle were adorned with bumblebee stickers, which the team had pasted on the walls of the factory as a not-so-serious advertising campaign for its design.

During the course of the 737 campaign, the Boeing team got the impression that history was about to repeat itself. At the end of the 1950s, airlines had to choose between the Boeing 707 and the Douglas DC-8. Now the choice was either to order DC-9s in different sizes or to order the Boeing 727 and 737 as a complete package.

On July 31, 1964, Jack E. Steiner presented the results to Boeing management. This was followed by a report to the Boeing Board of Directors on August 25 of that year. There was still no winner of the internal competition between the 737-242 (T tail), analyzed by Peyton Autry, and the 737-239 (with engines in nacelles beneath the wings), analyzed by Erik Lund. Both variants were technically feasible, but what was the future Boeing jet supposed to look like?

In the end, four basic arguments tipped the scales in favor of the now-familiar 737 configuration. First, weight could be saved by locating the engines under the wings, since a larger T tail requires more structure in the tail. Boeing engineers took advantage of this weight saving to use heavier yet more-powerful Pratt & Whitney JT8D engines. In addition, the reduced empty weight allowed the use of the 727 cabin cross section, and therefore the transport of more passengers in an aircraft of identical size.

The way was paved for the homogeneous aircraft family made up of the Boeing 707/720/727/737. Boeing promised that 17 percent of the aircraft structure, 64 percent of the equipment and 76 percent of the interior of the 727 and 737 would be identical. The basic layout of the flight decks of both types also differed only marginally—except for the third workstation for the flight engineer on board the 727.

In addition to Lufthansa, Boeing worked closely with United Air Lines on the design of the 737. Their engineers urged the manufacturer, for example, to bring the pressurized cabin as close to the tail as possible while maintaining a standing height. This maximization of the usable cabin floor, which allowed for the installation of an additional row of passenger seats, was a priority for United's engineers, which they had confirmed time and again on various visits to Seattle.

In October 1964, the configuration of the Boeing 737-100 had been finalized, but there was still no order—let alone a decision by Boeing management to build this aircraft type at all! The two key issues facing the Boeing board of directors on November 2, 1964, were how to avoid possible damage to the 727 program by an in-house competitor and how to minimize the expected costs of the new aircraft program. The latter point in particular was a headache for Boeing managers. And so a new calculation was worked out with the lowest possible costs, which might or might not have been correct. The program was presented to Boeing management on November 9, 1964, after which the 737 team was given permission to present the new model in detail to interested parties.

At the beginning of 1965, Boeing intensively tried to combine the different ideas of potential launch customers Eastern Air Lines, United Airlines, and Lufthansa in a final 737 design. Lufthansa sent a team to Renton in January to discuss the configuration desired by Lufthansa. Prof. Ernst Simon, long-standing head of the technical-projects department at Lufthansa, was particularly involved in the detailed planning. For example, the rear onboard passenger stairs of the 737 were his idea! Professor Simon recalls: "Boeing had its own design for an onboard, electrically operated staircase, which was too complicated in my opinion. A real technical monster! To integrate a staircase into the left rear door was not so easy due to the shape of the fuselage. But my idea for simple-to-use onboard passenger stairs for the 737 was well received by Boeing—and that is exactly what was built on the production line!"

As Jack E. Steiner believed, Simon's principal fear was that Eastern and United would insist on a larger variant of the 737-100, which was favored by Lufthansa. These fears were not entirely unfounded, since United was indeed anxious to obtain an aircraft from Boeing whose maximum size was limited only by the power from its two JT8D engines. This was a desire that eventually resulted in the 737-200, of which United ordered up to seventy-five.

At the beginning of 1965, the tone between Lufthansa and Boeing worsened. Lufthansa's chief technical officer, Gerhard Höltje, had been a strong advocate of the 737 for a long time and defended the project against in-house and political supporters of the alternative BAC 111 and Douglas DC9. He had personally campaigned so strongly for the 737 that a further delay or even cancellation of the project on the part of Boeing might have cost him his position—or at least severely damaged his reputation within Lufthansa. When the Boeing board met in New Orleans on February 1 to decide on the start of the program, Jack E. Steiner was aware of the explosive situation. A further delay would surely result in the loss of the Lufthansa order, which was thought to be secure. On that fateful day, Boeing president Bill Allen is said to have initially spoken out against the production of the 737, but other board members convinced him otherwise. At the end of the day, the 737 was officially launched and the sale to Lufthansa was approved. Shortly thereafter, on February 19, 1965, the Lufthansa supervisory board authorized the executive board to purchase twenty-one Boeing 737-130s and five additional Boeing 727-030s. The letter of agreement signed on the same day was followed on March 15, 1965, by the official signing of the contract between the two companies. The Boeing 737, the bestselling commercial aircraft of all time, was born!

In 1965, Lufthansa launched an internal search among its employees for a catchy name for its 737 fleet. The name Olympia Jet won but was overturned by an executive board resolution on March 28, 1967, in favor of City Jet, which is still in use today.

On April 9, 1967, the first Boeing 737-100 took off on its maiden flight at Boeing's Renton airfield, followed by the first 737-200 on August 8 of that year. After completion of the eight-month flight test program, which involved six aircraft that spent some 14,000 hours in the air, on December 15, 1967, both versions received US type certifications.

December 27, 1967, was a great day, and not just for Lufthansa's chief technical officer, Gerhard Höltje, when Boeing officially handed over the first 737 to the German airline at the Renton plant. After crew training at Seattle and Tucson, Arizona, Lufthansa celebrated the world premiere of the first scheduled flight of a Boeing on February 10, 1968.

The rest is history—and in the case of the Boeing 737, it would exceed the scope of this book. It is also historical fact that United Airlines and Western Airlines flew their Boeing 737-200s with a crew of three pilots in the early years, as demanded by the American pilots' union, because the maximum takeoff weight exceeded the 80,000 pounds mentioned earlier. Fortunately, aviation has made certain advances over the decades, not only on board the aircraft, but also in the thinking and actions of the people involved!

SPECIFICATIONS OF THE COMPETING TYPES

Type	Manufacturer	First Flight	Number Built	Wingspan	Length	Height	Power Plants	Cruise Speed	Range	Crew
Sud Aviation SE Caravelle (Swissair SE 210 III version)	Société Nationale de Construction Aéronautique du Sud-Est Aviation, Toulouse, France	May 27, 1955	282	112.5 ft.	105 ft.	28.6 ft.	2 × Rolls-Royce RA-29 Mk. 257	approx. 515.7 mph	approx. 1,830 mi.	2 pilots (cockpit)
Boeing 737 (Lufthansa Boeing 737-130)	Boeing Company, Seattle, Washington	Apr. 9, 1967	11.022 as of May 2022	93 ft.	94 ft.	37 ft.	2 × Pratt & Whitney JT8D-7	approx. 559 mph	approx. 1,317 mi.	2 pilots (cockpit)
BAC 111 (One Eleven)	Hunting Aircraft Ltd. / British Aircraft Corporation, Hurn, Great Britain	Aug. 20, 1963	244 (including nine ROMBAC 111)	88.5 ft.	93.5 ft.	24.6 ft.	2 × Rolls-Royce Spey Mk. 511	approx. 503 mph	approx. 2,249 mi.	2 pilots (cockpit)

CHAPTER 4
THE LEGENDS FLY ON

As part of their "Heavy Aircraft Training," the pilots of space shuttle mission STS-119 made several flights in the elderly DC-9 from Ellington Field, which is close to NASA's Johnson Space Center, Houston, Texas, which specializes in manned space projects. Here astronauts Lee Archambault (left) and Tony Antonelli, commander and pilot of the space shuttle STS-119 mission, pose in the cockpit of NASA's DC-9.

THE LAST DC-9S

While regular MD-80s and MD-90s are getting lesscommon, especially in the United States, in Africa and North America there are still a handful of DC-9 jets in daily service as passenger or cargo aircraft and research aircraft. Following is a list of the last DC-9 operators—some no longer in operation, others may resume service.

FLYING FOR NASA

The US space agency NASA used a DC-9-32 for so-called Zero G parabolic flights, which create weightless conditions on board the aircraft for a brief time at the zenith of the parabola. The passenger list mostly includes teams of researchers preparing weightlessness experiments for later setup on board the International Space Station (ISS). In addition, with the help of these NASA DC-9s, future astronauts are familiarized with the feeling of weightlessness and thus prepare them realistically for their later missions. The aircraft was originally delivered to the Dutch airline KLM in 1970 with the registration PH-DNZ. It subsequently served with the Venezuelan airline VIASA and then with the US Navy as a C-9B Skytrain II. It has been flying for NASA since 2004 and is currently in storage.

Built for KLM in 1970, the DC-9-32 was for many years in service as NASA's "Zero G" aircraft. These pictures of a parabolic flight were taken from a T-38 escort aircraft. During parabolic flights, weightlessness prevails on board for about twenty to thirty seconds—ideal space training. *NASA*

NASA
N932NA

Spectacular night launch of the space shuttle *Discovery* on March 15, 2009, beginning mission STS-119. The intensive preparation by the two space shuttle pilots included flights in the NASA DC-9. *NASA*

At the time tthe original German version of this book was written in 2018 book was written, the DC-9-10 shown here, originally delivered to Trans Canada Airlines in April 1966, was the oldest DC-9 still in regular service, having flown for 52.5 years! In this photo it is seen with a Douglas DC-3 Dakota of the American airline North Central on the Douglas factory ramp at Long Beach. Its last operator was the Nigerian airline Five Forty Aviation, which operated under the name Fly540. In the summer of 2022 the aircraft was stored.

KALITTA CHARTERS II

According to unconfirmed reports, four airlines were still flying DC-9-10s and DC-9-30s both in passenger and cargo versions in the United States in autumn 2017. Kalitta Charters II, based at Detroit Willow Run Airport, was one of them. In the autumn of 2017, Kalitta Charters II operated two DC-9-10Fs and a DC-9-32F on cargo flights, which were phased-out in July and December of 2019. A half-century-old DC-9-10s was delivered by Douglas to Continental Airline in 1967 and has since flown with Hughes Airwest and Republic Airlines. Converted into a freighter, it began its cargo career with the US express service Purolator Express, followed by Emery Worldwide and Reliant Airlines, before joining Kalitta Charters II fleet in 2003.

Source: Kalitta Charters II

Charters II

arters II

Kalitta Charters II
N915CK

Kalitta Charters II
N915CK

SKYDIVE PERRIS

Bennie Conatser, owner of California-based Skydive Perris, a commercial company that offers skydives from its fleet of aircraft, is the owner of a DC-9-21 with the current registration of N127NK.

It began its career with the Swedish registration SE-DBO and on May 1, 1969, was delivered to SAS as one of ten DC-9-21s built, with the serial number 488. After a hiatus of several years, in 2018 the aircraft was scheduled to be used as a drop plane for up to eighty parachutists per flight. The former SAS DC-9 is about halfway through its service life, with around 55,000 flight hours, and according to Bennie Conatser's plans, it will return to serve for many years to come.

Equipped with new engines, which were first tested in autumn 2017, the DC-9 was to serve as a jump aircraft for skydivers beginning in mid-2018. *Skydive Perris*

DC-9-21 Siger Viking during its service with SAS. *SAS*

The parachutists leave the aircraft by way of the modified rear door of the DC-9-21. *Skydive Perris*

The DC-9-21 making a low pass over the Skydive Perris base after dropping its parachutists. *Skydive Perris*

THE LAST EUROPEAN MD-80

Since Danish Air Transport phased out the last MD-80 in November 2021, in the summer of 2022, the Bulgarian airline European Air Charter was the last European operator of MD-80 aircraft.

DANISH AIR TRANSPORT

Danish Air Transport (DAT) was formed by Jesper and Kirsten Rungholm of Denmark in 1989, initially with a single Short SC-7 Skyvan. After initial contracts for the carriage of mail and a wide variety of cargo, including racehorses and equipment for the Paris-to-Dakar Rally, the airline grew over the years. Today it employs 340 people and has seventeen aircraft, including thirteen ATR Turboprops

EUROPEAN AIR CHARTER

In summer of 2022, the fleet operated by European Air Charter, based in Sofia, consisted of seven Airbus A320s and eight McDonnell Douglas MD-82 jets, taken over from defunct Bulgarian Air Charter in April 2021. The privately owned Bulgarian airline was founded in 2000 and flies tourists to the Bulgarian vacation region around Varna and Burgas on the Black Sea for a large number of European tour operators.

This colorfully painted MD-87, which DAT used to fly Danish tourists to the Mediterranean, has since been retired from service. *DAT*

Dramatic low-pass sequence by DAT MD-87 during the air show at Copenhagen-Roskilde airport in the summer of 2016. *DAT*

DAT began operating the MD-83 seen here, its sole example of this type, in autumn 2017. *DAT*

dat.dk

DOUGLAS DC-9 SPECIFICATIONS

Type	First Flight	Number Built	Wingspan	Length	Height	Engines	Cruise*	Range*	Crew
DC-9-10	2/25/1965	137	89.4 ft.	104.3 ft.	27.4 ft.	2 × Pratt & Whitney JT8D-1	522 mph	1,451 mi.	2 pilots
DC-9-21	9/21/1968	10	93.5 ft.	104.7 ft.	27.6 ft.	2 × Pratt & Whitney JT8D-11	506 mph	1,429 mi.	2 pilots
DC-9-41	11/28/1967	71	93.5 ft.	125.7 ft.	28.2 ft.	2 × Pratt & Whitney JT8D-11	506 mph	1,616 mi.	2 pilots
DC-9-51	12/17/1974	96	93.3 ft.	133.6 ft.	28 ft.	2 × Pratt & Whitney JT8D-17	497 mph	1,678 mi.	2 pilots
MD-82	1/8/1981	569	107.8 ft.	147.9 ft.	29.3 ft.	2 × Pratt & Whitney JT8D-217/-219	497 mph	2,050 mi.	2 pilots
DC-9-32	8/1/1967	662 (incl. military variant)	93.3 ft.	119 ft.	27.5 ft.	2 × Pratt & Whitney JT8D-9	497 mph	1,678 mi.	2 pilots
MD-88	8/15/1987	150	107.8 ft.	147.9 ft.	29.3 ft.	2 × Pratt & Whitney JT8D-217C	497 mph	2,050 mi.	2 pilots
DC-9-81 (MD-81)	10/18/1979	132	107.8 ft.	147.9 ft.	29.3 ft.	2 × Pratt & Whitney JT8D-209	497 mph	2,050 mi.	2 pilots
MD-83	12/17/1984	265	107.8 ft.	147.9 ft.	29.3 ft.	2 × Pratt & Whitney JT8D-219	497 mph	2,050 mi.	2 pilots
MD-87	12/4/1986	75	107.6 ft.	130.4 ft.	30.5 ft.	2 × Pratt & Whitney JT8D-219B/C	497 mph	2,050 mi.	2 pilots
MD-90-30	2/22/1993	117	107.84 ft.	149.4 ft.	29.3 ft.	2 × IAE V2525-D5	497 mph	2,610 mi.	2 pilots
McDonnell Douglas MD-95	9/2/1998	156	93.3 ft.	124 ft.	29.1 ft.	2 × Rolls-Royce BR 715	497 mph	1,615 mi.	2 pilots

THE AUTHOR
WOLFGANG BORGMANN

Wolfgang Borgmann's enthusiasm for aviation was passed on to him by his parents, who were active in the aviation field. In his early years, he began building up an aviation historical collection that provides numerous rare photos and documents, as well as exciting background information, for his books. Since 1995, Borgmann has been active as an aviation journalist and since 2008 as an author. He lives in Oerlinghausen, Germany. His website is www.aerojournalist.de.

SCHIFFER BOOKS *on Related Subjects*

SCHIFFER PUBLISHING

Boeing 737
A Legends of Flight Illustrated History
ISBN: 978-0-7643-6138-8 $29.99

Airbus A300/310
A Legends of Flight Illustrated History
ISBN: 978-0-7643-6139-5 $29.99

McDonnell Douglas DC-10/MD-11
A Legends of Flight Illustrated History
ISBN: 978-0-7643-6137-1 $$29.99

Boeing 757
A Legends of Flight Illustrated History
ISBN: 978-0-7643-6346-7 $29.99

N900RF
NASA